PENGUIN BOOK
THE OLD MAN AND HIS GOD

Sudha Murty was born in 1950 in Shiggaon in north Karnataka. An M.Tech in Computer Science, she teaches Computer Science to postgraduate students. She is also the chairperson of the Infosys Foundation. A prolific writer in English and Kannada, she has written nine novels, four technical books, three travelogues, one collection of short stories and two collections of non-fiction pieces, including *How I Taught My Grandmother to Read and Other Stories* (Puffin 2004). Her books have been translated into all the major Indian languages and have sold over 150,000 copies.

THE OLD MAN AND HIS GOD

DISCOVERING THE SPIRIT OF INDIA

SUDHA MURTY

PENGUIN BOOKS

PENGUIN BOOKS
Published by the Penguin Group
Penguin Books India Pvt. Ltd, 11 Community Centre, Panchsheel Park, New
Delhi 110 017, India
Penguin Group (USA) Inc., 375 Hudson Street, New York, New York 10014,
USA
Penguin Group (Canada), 90 Eglinton Avenue East, Suite 700, Toronto,
Ontario, M4P 2Y3, Canada (a division of Pearson Penguin Canada Inc.)
Penguin Books Ltd, 80 Strand, London WC2R 0RL, England
Penguin Ireland, 25 St Stephen's Green, Dublin 2, Ireland (a division of Penguin
Books Ltd)
Penguin Group (Australia), 250 Camberwell Road, Camberwell, Victoria
3124, Australia (a division of Pearson Australia Group Pty Ltd)
Penguin Group (NZ), cnr Airborne and Rosedale Roads, Albany, Auckland
1310, New Zealand (a division of Pearson New Zealand Ltd)
Penguin Group (South Africa) (Pty) Ltd, 24 Sturdee Avenue, Rosebank,
Johannesburg 2196, South Africa

Penguin Books Ltd, Registered Offices: 80 Strand, London WC2R 0RL,
England

First published by Penguin Books India 2006

Copyright © Sudha Murty 2006

10

ISBN-13: 978-0-14400-101-9   ISBN-10: 0-14400-101-2

Typeset in Sabon by Mantra Virtual Services, New Delhi
Printed at Baba Barkhanath Printers, Bahadurgarh, Haryana

For Infosys Foundation, that has shown me a world beyond, with immense gratitude

Contents

PREFACE ix

1. THE OLD MAN AND HIS GOD 1

2. FREEDOM OF SPEECH 5

3. HOREGALLU 11

4. THE WAY YOU LOOK AT IT 15

5. A TALE OF TWO BROTHERS 18

6. THE JOURNEY 24

7. AN OFFICEGOER'S DILEMMA 30

8. THE DESERVING CANDIDATE 35

9. THE BUSINESS OF PHILANTHROPY 40

10. A HELPING HAND 45

11. TRUE SHADES OF NATURE 52

12. MADE IN HEAVEN 58

13. THE GRATEFUL TENANT   62

14. A FOREIGNER, ALWAYS   67

15. THE LINE OF
    SEPARATION   70

16. A BUDDHIST ON AIRPORT
    ROAD   78

17. SWEET HOSPITALITY   83

18. FRIENDS FOREVER   87

19. THE PERFECT LIFE   92

20. HUNDRED PER CENT
    FREE   97

21. TWO FACES OF
    POVERTY   101

22. INDIA, THE HOLY LAND   107

23. MOTHER'S LOVE   112

24. VILLAGE ENCOUNTERS   117

25. MAY YOU BE THE MOTHER
    OF A HUNDRED
    CHILDREN   121

PREFACE

I have now written two collections of my real-life experiences which many say they have enjoyed reading. This is my third. All the experiences mentioned here are real, though the names have been changed in some places. People often ask me how it is that so many interesting things happen only to me. To them I reply that in life's journey we all meet strange people and undergo so many experiences that touch us and sometimes even change us. If you have a sensitive mind and record your observations regularly, you will see your life too is a vast storehouse of stories.

Of course there are some incidents here which happened to me because of the people I met during my work or in my travels. In all the cases I have taken care to take the permission of the people I have written about.

I have often wondered what it is about these experiences that has been appreciated by readers in all corners of the country. I have come to the conclusion that it is because they are told simply and are all true. After all, there is something within all of us that attracts us to the truth. I have tried to hold up a mirror to the lives of the people of our country and attempted to trace that spirit within us which makes us uniquely Indian.

I have dedicated this book to the Infosys Foundation. For many, the foundation is a charitable organization, a branch of a rich company. But for me, it is something closest to my heart. Initially I was a mother to it. I was there from the day it came into existence. Somewhere along the line, it has become the mother and I the child. Holding its hands, I have journeyed many miles, faced praise and criticism. It has been an integral part of my life. We have never abandoned each other.

There are many people who have worked with me in the long journey that a book undergoes from the time it leaves the writer's desk. I would like to thank them all. I want to thank Sudeshna Shome Ghosh of Penguin India, for her efforts, without which the book would not have been published.

The royalty proceeds from this book will go to charity.

November 2005   Sudha Murty
                                                Bangalore

THE OLD MAN AND HIS GOD

A few years back, I was travelling in the Thanjavur district of Tamil Nadu. It was getting dark, and due to a depression over the Bay of Bengal, it was raining heavily. The roads were overflowing with water and my driver stopped the car near a village. 'There is no way we can proceed further in this rain,' said the driver. 'Why don't you look for shelter somewhere nearby rather than sit in the car?'

Stranded in an unknown place among unknown people, I was a bit worried. Nevertheless, I retrieved my umbrella and marched out into the pelting rain. I started walking towards the tiny village, whose name I cannot recall now. There was no electricity and it was a trial walking in the darkness and the rain. In the distance I could just make out the shape of a small temple. I decided it would be an ideal place to take shelter, so I made my way to it. Halfway there, the rain started coming down even more fiercely and the strong wind blew my umbrella away, leaving me completely drenched. I reached the temple soaking wet. As soon as I entered, I heard an elderly person's voice calling out to me. Though I cannot speak Tamil, I could make out the concern in the voice. In the course of my travels, I have come to realize that voices from the heart can be understood irrespective of the language they speak.

I peered into the darkness of the temple and saw an old man of about eighty. Standing next to him was an equally old lady in a traditional nine-yard cotton sari. She said something to him and then approached me with a worn but clean towel in her hand. As I wiped my face and head I noticed that the man was blind. It was obvious from their surroundings that they were very poor. The Shiva temple, where I now stood, was simple with the minimum of ostentation in its decorations. The Shivalinga was bare except for a bilwa leaf on top. The only light came from a single oil lamp. In that flickering light a sense of calm overcame me and I felt myself closer to god than ever before.

In halting Tamil, I asked the man to perform the evening mangalarati, which he did with love and dedication. When he finished, I placed a hundred-rupee note as the dakshina.

He touched the note and pulled away his hand, looking uncomfortable. Politely he said, 'Amma, I can make out that the note is not for ten rupees, the most we usually receive. Whoever you may be, in a temple, your devotion is important, not your money. Even our ancestors have said that a devotee should give as much as he or she can afford to. To me you are a devotee of Shiva, like everyone else who comes here. Please take back this money.'

I was taken aback. I did not know how to react. I looked at the man's wife expecting her to argue with him and urge him to take the money, but she just stood quietly.

Often, in many households, a wife encourages the man's greediness. Here, it was the opposite. She was endorsing her husband's views. So I sat down with them, and with the wind and rain whipping up a frenzy outside, we talked about our lives. I asked them about themselves, their life in the village temple and whether they had anyone to look after them.

Finally I said, 'Both of you are old. You don't have any children to look after your everyday needs. In old age one requires more medicines than groceries. This village is far from any of the towns in the district. Can I suggest something to you?'

At that time, we had started an old-age pension scheme and I thought, looking at their worn-out but clean clothes, they would be the ideal candidates for it.

This time the wife spoke up, 'Please do tell, child.'

'I will send you some money. Keep it in a nationalized bank or post office. The interest on that can be used for your monthly needs. If there is a medical emergency you can use the capital.'

The old man smiled on hearing my words and his face lit up brighter than the lamp.

'You sound much younger than us. You are still foolish. Why do I need money in this great old age? Lord Shiva is also known as Vaidyanathan. He is the Mahavaidya, or great doctor. This village we live in has many kind people. I perform the pooja and they give me rice in return. If either of us is unwell, the local doctor gives us medicines. Our wants are very few. Why would I accept money from an unknown person? If I keep this money in the bank, like you are telling me to, someone will come to know and may harass us. Why should I take on these worries? You are a kind person to offer help to two unknown old people. But we are content; let us live as we always have. We don't need anything more.'

Just then the electricity came back and a bright light lit up the temple. For the first time I saw the couple properly. I could clearly see the peace and happiness on their faces. They were the first people I met who refused help in spite of their obvious need. I did not agree with everything he had just said, but it was clear to me that his contentment had brought him peace. Such an attitude may not let you progress fast, but after a certain period in life it is required. Perhaps this world with its many stresses and strains has much to learn from an old couple in a forgettable corner of India.

FREEDOM OF SPEECH

Alka and I have been friends since the time we were in school and college together. Alka was the star debater of our university. Her arguments, bold, convincing and razor sharp, usually left her opponents floundering. She was called the 'Queen of Speech' by her friends.

Even after college and through our years of marriage and children, we continued to keep in touch. Alka married a mechanical engineer and settled down in Bombay in a beautiful flat on the Worli sea face. Her husband started his own small-scale industry and they were very well off. She had a daughter who got married and went to live in the US. Alka herself went on to become the head of the sociology department in a good college. I always thought of her as having the perfect life.

Once, I had to go to Bombay on some work, and Alka invited me to stay with her. There I met Tulsi, her efficient maid. Tulsi was from the Maharashtra-Karnataka border and spoke the same language as Alka and me. Drought and poverty had forced many families from that region to emigrate to larger cities in search of work. Most ended up as construction workers on daily wages, yet they never lost the hope of being able to save enough money to go back to their villages.

Tulsi too had come to Bombay in search of work, but had settled down here. She had worked in Alka's house for many years and was an asset due to her hardworking nature, punctuality and reliability.

One day, during my visit, Tulsi did not come for work at her usual time. As the clock ticked away, Alka was getting more and more agitated. She had to attend and also speak at an international sociology conference. She had become so used to Tulsi that she could not do anything on her own, though I knew, long back, she used to be a good cook. That is what efficient maids and secretaries do to you at home and in the office.

I was watching her agitation and could not help laughing. This upset her even more. She said, 'It is easy for you to laugh. But you don't know how much I have helped her out in her times of need. How could she do this to me on such a busy day? She knows I have some very important work today. You do not realize the responsibility I have been given in this seminar. You take things too easy. That is why you have remained only a visiting professor.'

I did not get upset at Alka's remarks. After all, we had been friends for long, and had always been very frank with each other. And what she had said was also the truth, which few other people could have said to me.

So instead of laughing, I offered a different solution.

'Alka, why can't we go to Tulsi's house and find out what is causing the delay? There is no point in fuming and increasing your blood pressure.'

I knew Tulsi stayed in a slum just across the road. In a city like Bombay, where rich people stay in beautiful apartments, there are double the number staying in adjoining slums. In fact, these slums have become essential for the survival of the residents of the big apartment blocks. Reluctantly, Alka agreed with my suggestion and we walked across the road to Tulsi's house.

As we approached her house, we heard the sound of voices raised in argument. Some people were quarrelling very loudly. We turned a corner and were surprised to behold the sight of Tulsi berating someone. She was screaming at a man standing quietly near by. Alka whispered to me that it was Raman, Tulsi's husband. His wife was showering the choicest of abuses at him and he was standing with his head bent low. In her extreme agitation, Tulsi was talking in her native dialect. She was so furious I would not have been surprised if she landed a few blows on him as well. Her neighbours were going about their work but were giving sympathetic glances in her direction from time to time. Tulsi finally saw us and calmed down slightly.

'Tulsi, don't use such language. You can solve the problem without bad words. What is the matter? Be cool and tell me what has happened.' I asked her in our language.

By this time Tulsi managed to control her emotions and breaking into tears she replied, 'Amma, with such difficulty I had saved some money and bought a pair of gold bangles and a chain for myself. It was with my own hard-earned money. And do you know what this fellow has done? He has gone and mortgaged them in order to start a paan shop. Is it fair? How can you ask me to be cool? They were my life's savings. I know Alka amma has some important work today but I could not control my anger when he told me this in the morning.'

I stood and consoled her for some time. My work involves talking to many people like her, who are grappling with basic day-to-day survival issues and have nothing to do with the glitz and glamour that many of us take for granted. In any case, being a teacher, I am quite used to giving sermons, whether they are wanted or not.

As we walked back home, Alka was very quiet. I assumed she was worried thinking of all the household work piled up for her. Affectionately I said, 'Don't worry about the cooking and other work. I'll help you now and I am sure Tulsi will be back in the evening. These people talk freely about their feelings and hence forget fast too. I bet by tonight Tulsi will have made up with her husband and may even go off to watch a movie with him.'

By this time we had entered the flat and I made my way to the kitchen to wash the vessels. I am not a very good cook, but I am definitely proficient in washing up. Alka said she would make some tea for us and went to the other corner of the kitchen. To my surprise after a while I heard sounds of sobbing coming from her. She was trying hard to suppress them but the tears were coming down fast.

I walked up to her and laid a hand on her shoulder. The moment I touched her, Alka broke down and started crying openly.

'Alka, please don't be so upset. You should not be so sensitive about what happened to Tulsi . . .'

'I am not worried about Tulsi. I have just realized today that my state is worse than hers.'

I was stunned at her words. She went on, 'It took a great deal of effort for us to buy this flat. You realize how expensive it is, and I gave every paisa from my salary towards the payment. This flat represents my life's savings. But do you know what my husband did? One day, when he was not here, there was a registered letter for him from the bank. I opened it to find that he has mortgaged the flat, which we bought in his name for income tax reasons, to the bank. His business was not doing well and he needed extra money desperately. But he did all this without telling me anything. I was furious. If we lose this flat where shall we go? But we live in "civilized" society, so I could not shout and scream at him. I could not raise my voice and abuse him as the neighbours would then know we were fighting. I have been keeping all this anger inside me for a long time. Tulsi is better off than me. At least she has the freedom to shout at her husband and even hit him if she is angry and then forget about it. I have to live with the hurt festering inside me forever.'

I did not know what to say to her. Helplessly I stared out at the sea from her beautiful balcony. The images I had in my mind about Alka from our schooldays as a bold, confident orator lay ruined. She was nothing but an ordinary, meek, ineffectual woman, unable to stand up to her husband and fight for her rights. To change the subject

I asked her, 'What are you going to speak about at the seminar today?'

Ironically, the answer came, 'Freedom of speech.'

HOREGALLU

Hot summer days remind me of my childhood in a little village. There was a large banyan tree right in the middle of the village, and I would spend many hours playing under it during my holidays. The tree was like a massive umbrella with its branches providing much needed shade and succour. Travellers spent some time sitting under it and catching their breath before going on their way. To make them comfortable there was a 'horegallu' under the tree. Horegallu literally means 'a stone that can bear weight'. It was a large flat stone placed horizontally over two vertical ones, thus making a stone bench on which anyone could sit and rest awhile, chat with a fellow traveller and exchange news of the road. Cool water would be kept in earthern pots near the bench and people could quench their thirst before starting their journeys again. I am sure similar simple arrangements can be found in villages all over the country.

The horegallu in our village holds special memories for me as it is inextricably linked with my grandfather. He was a retired schoolteacher and would spend hours every day sitting under the banyan tree and talking to those resting there. When I would get tired of playing I would sit next to him and observe the people he was speaking to and listen to their conversations. Most of them were villagers taking a break from their work in the fields nearby. They had to walk long distances each day carrying heavy burdens on their heads. Tired out by the heat, they would drink the cool water, wash their faces with it and chat with Grandfather. Their conversation would be about their daily lives and worries.

'Masterji, this summer has been so hot. I have never seen such dry weather.' Or, 'Masterji, it is getting difficult for me to carry these large loads on my head. Thank god for this horegallu. I wish my son would help, but he only wants to go to the city . . .' They spoke about the difficulties they lived with. My grandfather could only listen to them but just talking to him seemed to refresh them for the journey. After some time they would pick up their burdens with some ease and go on their way. The horegallu was an important feature in their lives and as a child I would often not understand why they blessed it so often for being there. After all it was only a stone bench. It was my grandfather who told me, 'Child, a horegallu is essential in any journey. We all carry our burdens according to our situations and capacities. But every once in a while we need to stop, put down that burden and rest. Only then can we be refreshed enough to pick up the load once more. The horegallu gives everyone that opportunity to do so. It helps people regain their strengths.'

Later on in life, I got to see something that reminded me of that stone bench once again. I was working in Bombay. One of my colleagues Ratna was a senior clerk, middle aged and always smiling. She had done her graduation and been working in the company for nearly twenty-five years. She went about her repetitive, mundane work with an infectious cheerfulness.

Every day, during the lunch hour she would sit with some person in one of the rooms, and they would have long chats. I would often wonder what they talked about. One day, I finally asked her, 'Ratna, what do you talk with each person for the whole lunch hour?'

Ratna smiled and said simply, 'They share their troubles with me.'

'But how can you solve the troubles of so many people? Do you always have an answer for them?'

'No, I only listen.'

'And that is enough? That solves the problem?' I was young and incredulous at such a simplistic outlook. But Ratna answered with the same patience and affection that she must have used with all my colleagues, 'I am not a trained counsellor or an intellectual. No one can solve your problem. You have to do it yourself.'

'Then how do you help them by listening to them?'

'God has given me two ears to listen to others. I hear them out with sympathy and without any judgement. When a person in trouble or under a lot of strain finds an outlet for his worries, it relieves half his burden.'

I thought for sometime and said, 'But don't you ever break the confidence and tell others the secrets you hear, even by mistake?'

'Not even in my dreams. I consider that to be the worst kind of betrayal. I don't think there is a greater sin than betraying someone's confidence. They tell me their worries because they know I will never talk about it or gossip about it to another person. Only when they know their words are secure with me, can they talk to me freely. This way I relieve their burden for a short while till they are ready to pick themselves up and carry on with their journey.'

Her words uncannily echoed my grandfather's, sitting on the stone bench under the banyan tree. Perhaps, in their own small ways, without access to great wealth, both these people were doing some tremendous social service. No one thought of acknowledging their work or rewarding them for it, but they continued to do so, as these small acts of kindness gave them joy. If ever now I happen to pass a horegallu in a village, I remember them and wish there were many more of them in this world.

The Way You Look at It

A few years ago, I was travelling to a village in Karnataka on some work. I had got delayed and it was getting dark. There were no lights on the road and I was anxious to get to my destination. As we neared the outskirts of the village, the beams of the car's headlights picked out some shrubs on the side of the road. They were thorny shrubs and to my astonishment I saw many women coming out from behind them, shyly covering their heads, each with a tin box in hand. I realized they had gone there to attend to nature's call.

Soon I reached the village headman, Veerappa's house. He was a wealthy man and had arranged an elaborate dinner for me, with many courses including a few different types of sweets. The food was delicious, but my mind was not in enjoying it. I could not get the image of the women skulking out from behind the shrubs out of my mind.

When at last dinner was over, I asked to meet the cook. She was an elderly lady called Sharanamma. She was very shy and talked to me in a low voice. I wanted to know her better, so I said, 'The food was excellent. Can I give you something in return?'

Shyly she replied, 'Amma, I have heard you do a lot of

work for poor people. If possible can you build some public toilets for the women of this village? Life is very difficult for us. Unlike men, we cannot go for our toilet in the day. Like thieves we have to wait till it is dark, then we have to go behind bushes, that too in groups. Whenever a vehicle passes us on the main road and the car's lights fall on us we feel ashamed. And if ever we are unwell and need to go in the middle of the night then heaven help us. This is particularly traumatic for the young girls. We all would be very happy if you could do something about this.'

I was amazed at Sharanamma's sense of responsibility towards her community. I turned to Veerappa and said it was a shame that the headmen of the village had not thought it important that their women should answer nature's call with dignity and in privacy. It is a basic right that should be available to every human being. Finally I told him, 'I am ready to build these toilets for the village if you will maintain them well.' Veerappa, already ashamed after my tirade, readily agreed.

Thus started our foundation's work to build public toilets in the countryside and in key areas in Bangalore. In India people are usually enthusiastic about building temples, mosques and gurudwaras, but no one thinks it important to build something as essential as a toilet. Perhaps because there is no *punya* attached to it.

The toilets that we built in Bangalore were pay-and-use ones. Though many people objected to having to pay, this was one way we could ensure their cleanliness and proper maintenance.

One day, I went to visit the first toilet, near a busy bus-stand in the city. It was an unplanned visit and I stood behind two women as they waited to go in. They looked like working women and regular commuters on one of the buses. Suddenly I heard them mention my name. 'This Sudha Murty is a really mean lady. When she has spent so much money constructing this, why has she made it pay-and-use?' The other one replied. 'You are right. You don't know about her. I have heard from people that she has built many toilets in Bangalore and she is running some trust with the help of toilet money. She must be making a huge profit.'

I was shocked at their words. Even if one tries to do something to improve a city's civic life, people make all kinds of strange comments. For a while I was upset. Then I cooled down and told myself that people may say whatever they like, but I had to do what I had decided on. I know that the public toilets have benefitted many like Sharanamma. What she had perceived to be an act of necessity for the village women, was looked at here by these two women, as a business venture.

After all, life is the way you look at it.

A Tale of Two Brothers

Ram and Shyam were identical twins and my students in pre-university and graduate college where they studied for an MCA degree. This meant I taught them for nearly seven years. Obviously, I got to know them and their family quite well in the course of those years. Like many other twins I have known, Ram and Shyam were happy in each other's company and always stayed together in college, sharing homework, lab and class notes. They looked so similar that at times I could not make out which was Ram and which Shyam. 'You should wear something so I can make out one from the other!' I would joke with them. 'I get so confused. What will happen after you get married? Perhaps you should marry identical twins too, then there will be great fun and confusion all around.'

After they completed their MCA degree, they joined a software company. Their father was an industrialist and their mother the principal of a school. They were therefore from an affluent family and owned a large house and a farmhouse. One day, the two young men came to invite me to their wedding. Funnily, they were indeed getting married to two sisters who were also twins!

'It seems like your life story will be like a film script!' I joked again. 'How did you find the twin girls? What are their names?'

'Madam, when we decided to get married we deliberately looked around for twins, as we felt only another pair of twins would be able to understand us and our friendship completely. Their names are Smita and Savita. You must come to our wedding. After all, this was first your idea!'

I did attend the wedding and blessed the two couples wholeheartedly. I felt it must be a great relief for the two sets of parents as well. The two brothers marrying two sisters meant there was not going to be any rivalry between the two couples.

Many months later, out of the blue, Ram and Shyam's mother called me one day. She sounded tired. 'Madam can you come and talk to the children?' she asked wearily.

I could sense there was some problem, and that weekend itself, I went to their house to find out what was the matter. For a while, I was unable to recognize the house, though I was standing right in front of it. Now there were two front doors instead of one and the garden was partitioned into two. I decided I had the wrong address or perhaps they had moved out, but Ram's mother saw me and called out from inside.

I stepped in and immediately sensed an awkwardness and sadness in the air. The house had been partitioned in a bizarre manner. The drawing room was now small, the bedrooms too large and the kitchen in an odd shape. A brick wall ran down the length of the house, from the hall to the kitchen. There was pin drop silence inside. I turned to their mother, 'What happened? Why have you put this wall here?' She told me the sad story.

'Ram and Shyam fought and separated, that is why this wall has come up. Why are you looking so surprised? People change when they grow up. They lose the innocence we saw in them when they were young boys.'

I said, 'Siblings often fight with each other because of their partners, but here they were sisters, so how could they instigate it?'

'We too had the same thoughts when we got them married. For a while things went well. After my husband retired, we decided to divide up the property and give equal shares to the brothers. That's when the trouble started. They both wanted the same house, the same farmhouse. How could we solve such a problem? They were adamant, and we ended up building this wall to separate the two households.'

That old saying is so true, money is one thing which rarely unites and mostly divides people. The quarrel was due to property.

Their mother wanted me to speak to them and advise them as their teacher. But I knew that in money matters there was little the words of their college teacher would change. I tried any way. I said, 'From the time you were conceived you have shared the same space. You shared your mother's womb, you grew up together in this house, sharing your joys and sorrows. You married twins so they would understand your friendship better. You must understand that in life sometimes it is important to compromise and live in peace with loved ones.'

They had no answer to my words and I knew I was talking to deaf ears. I went away, unsuccessful. By the time I reached home, I was late for a dinner appointment with an old friend. He was a colleague of mine and I had known him for many years. Seeing me walk in late, he said, 'You know, punctuality is the sign of a good teacher—not only to the class but elsewhere too.'

I agreed and apologized.

'I am sorry. But which restaurant are we going to now?'

His wife smiled and said, 'We are going to a village thirty kilometers away.'

'Oh, is it in a farmhouse?'

'No, we don't have a farmhouse. The dinner is at a farmer's house.'

I did not understand what they were talking about, so I quietly got into their car. My friend first drove us to the nearest market. There he bought sweets and fruits while his wife got some clothes. Curiously, I asked again, 'Where are we going?'

He coolly replied, 'To my brother's house. He has been asking us to visit him for a long time. I am sure you will like it there.' As far as I knew he did not have any brother or sister. He was the only child of his parents.

'Where has this brother turned up from? Is he a cousin? Or a close friend who is like a brother? Or like in Hindi films, have you suddenly discovered you have a long-lost brother?'

He only chose to smile mysteriously and drove on. Soon we were outside Bangalore and the car was moving fast on the highway. His silence disconcerted me and I wondered if I had asked too many questions and intruded upon his personal life. If we were in America and I had talked so much, he would have told me to shut up and mind my own business. But here in India we cannot resist asking questions about someone's personal life, whether we are interested or not.

Suddenly my friend started talking.

'Fifty-five years ago, I was born in the village we are going to visit. I lost my mother when I was only ten days old. My father had loved her immensely and was broken-hearted but he also had to look after me. I was allergic to cow's milk and with my mother dead I could not drink any milk. I would cry piteously the whole day in hunger. As you know, those days there was no infant formula or powdered milk. I started getting weaker and weaker and hopes for my survival started dwindling. My father was worried but did not know what to do. Help came to him in the form of Seetakka. She was the wife of our servant and had delivered a baby boy only a few days before I was born. Unable to bear my plight, she requested my father, "Anna, if you don't mind, I want to feed this baby my milk along with my son." My father thought for a while, and even though many relatives protested at the arrangement, he agreed and Seetakka saved my life by giving me her milk. She continued to feed me till I developed resistance to cow's milk and other food. I stayed for five years in this village before moving on to other places. But I always remember her and consider her to be a great woman. In fact, I look upon her son Hanuma as my brother. I gave him a part of my share of the property even though my relatives opposed the idea as usual. For them Seetakka was just a servant, but for me she was a large-hearted, simple woman, whose love knew no bounds.

'I am busy in Bangalore now, but I make it a point to visit her son, my brother, at least once a year. After all Seetakka poured her love on us in equal measure without expecting anything in return. We shared the love of the same mother, and that makes us brothers.'

By the time his story ended, we had reached the village and my friend pointed out Hanuma, waiting at the street corner to escort us to his house. All through dinner, watching the love between them, I was remembering the wall between Ram and Shyam's families and wondering at the quirks of destiny, which turned brothers into strangers and the sons of masters and servants into brothers.

Way back in 1974, before Infosys was even a gleam in our eyes, young Narayan Murthy was working as a team member in SESA, a French firm which was building software for handling air cargo at the then newly built Charles De Gaulle Airport in Paris. He was very shy and an idealist.

The money was good, and whatever remained after sending back home to fulfil his various family obligations, he donated to organizations working for the development of our country. His views tended to be leftist and he was an ardent believer in the principles of Marxism. After working in France for a few years, he wanted to come back to India. But unlike the other young Indian engineers, he decided to hitchhike his way back from Paris to Kabul. Carrying his backpack, he took rides in cars and trains, or simply walked when nothing was available. Little did he know when he set out, that this backpack journey would change his destiny, as well as affect many other lives!

One wintry Sunday morning, hitchhiking from an Italian town, he reached Nis, a border town between what was then Yugoslavia and Bulgaria. Once inside the communist block, Murthy realized it was not going to be easy to get rides from passing motorists, so he decided to take a train to Sofia, the capital of Bulgaria. Thus, on reaching Nis, he straightaway walked to the local railway station. His efforts at buying breakfast at the restaurant were not successful since they would not accept the Italian currency he was carrying and the banks were closed. Murthy slept off on the platform till eight p.m., when the Sofia Express arrived at Nis. The train generally stopped there for about two hours to handle the immigration chores. Murthy got on to the train and took his seat. To his delight, the compartment was nearly empty. Being an introvert, he was quite happy to be alone.

As he sat reading a book, a tall, blonde and beautiful girl entered the compartment and settled down in the adjacent seat. Murthy remained buried in his book and did not even bother to exchange a smile. Usually women, anywhere on earth, are talkative, and the girl broke the ice and struck up a conversation with him. When she got to know that he was from India, which then was much in favour of communism and socialism, the conversation naturally veered towards their countries' various policies. Slowly, they began talking about their personal lives as well. The girl explained her situation.

'I am from Sofia. I was sent on a scholarship by the government to Kiev University to do my PhD. There I met a nice young man from East Berlin. We liked each other and decided to get married.' Saying this much, she sighed.

'What was the matter? Why did you not get married?'

Murthy asked sympathetically.

'We did get married and that was the problem. We applied for permission to marry a citizen of another country to our respective governments. They agreed, except that Bulgaria wanted me to complete the term of my bond in my country and my husband was asked to stay back in East Germany for the same period. The result is I travel to East Germany once in six months while my husband comes to Sofia once in six months. This has become extremely frustrating for both of us. We have lost all hopes of leading a normal married life,' she said.

Murthy was touched by this predicament. He said, 'It is an unfair system. Whether it is a communist or a capitalist country, issues like the choice of partner for marriage, or job, and the freedom of expression should not be curtailed . . .'

All this time, a boy was sitting next to the girl. He had tried talking to her but she had not been interested. Murthy and the girl were conversing in French, and the boy had not been able to understand much of what they were talking. After listening to them for a while, the boy disappeared and came back with two burly, fierce-looking gentlemen. Without uttering a word, one of them caught Murthy by his shirt collar and dragged him on to the platform. The other person took the girl away.

Murthy was locked up in a small, dingy room with hardly any ventilation. There was no furniture or heating and only a crude toilet in one corner. He sat down on the floor in a daze. What had happened? Why was he locked up like a criminal? What had happened to the girl?

Gradually he figured it was the discussion on rights and duties of citizens in a communist country that had upset the boy and the cops.

'What will they do to me now? If something happens to me, will my family ever come to know?' he thought desperately. The very thought of his family in Mysore made him go weak with worry. His father was retired and recently struck by paralysis. He had to help his family in getting his three younger sisters married.

Hours passed by. He was not aware whether it was day or night. His wristwatch had been taken away along with his passport and other possessions. He had not eaten anything in over ninety hours. He could hear several trains come and go. After what seemed like an eternity, the door opened and Murthy was dragged on to the platform, put on a train along with a guard and told that his passport would be returned only after he reached Istanbul.

'What was my offence?' Murthy asked the policeman, holding the door of the compartment.

The stone-faced sergeant said, 'Why did you talk against the State? Who was the girl?'

'She was just a traveller like me . . .'

'Then why did she discuss her personal matters with you?' another sergeant immediately raised his voice, not even allowing Murthy to finish his sentence.

'What is wrong in that?' Murthy protested.

'It is against the rules of our country to discuss such issues', the sergeant replied firmly.

Murthy was curious about the girl's fate, 'What happened to her?'

'It is none of your business. We have checked your passport. It is only because you are from India, which is a friendly country, that we are releasing you. Don't try to do anything smart on the way. Just leave our country without any further mischief,' said the first sergeant, forcing him to get in and slamming the door.

The train started moving.

Murthy was tired. He had not eaten or slept in four days. He managed to sit down at a window seat. He was again on a train but things had changed dramatically. Murthy had enjoyed discussing and arguing passionately about the ideals of Karl Marx, Lenin, Mao and Ho Chi Minh sitting at the beautiful roadside cafés of Paris. They were theoretical discussions done on a full stomach. But now, hungry and overwrought after his brush with a communist state, Murthy had to rethink all his ideals. So this was what it was like to live behind the Iron Curtain! The system dealt with ruthless efficiency even a single voice raised against it. It denied basic freedom to its citizens and treated travellers from friendly countries thus. He shuddered to think what might have happened to him if he were from a capitalist country. Watching the countryside go by, Murthy realized the value of freedom. He also realized that the only way to get rid of poverty was not by raising slogans or issuing diktats, but by creating more and more jobs. He vowed then and there to himself that he would generate wealth not only for himself but for many others, legally and ethically. He would see that India was known through the world not for her poverty but for the skills of her young people—

that would be his contribution towards removing India's problems.

Armed with this new resolve, after returning to India he experimented with various jobs at different companies. He started his own small company Softronics for a while and went on to head the software division at Patni Computer Systems. But his greatest desire was to build an export-focussed company, with his values.

Finally, in 1981 he started Infosys.

The communist Murthy, over a period of time, changed to what he refers to now as a socialist capitalist.

The rest is history.

7

An Officegoer's Dilemma

In the numerous software companies setting up office in Bangalore, the issue of corporate social responsibility is being increasingly taken seriously. I was once invited to speak on this to the employees of one such company. Like most other offices this one too resembled a five star hotel, with its marble and granite floors, chandeliers, paintings on the walls, the housekeepers sweeping and mopping incessantly and an extremely polite front office.

I usually follow my talks with a question-answer session. I consider that the litmus test of how well my talk has been received. I have a theory that if people do not ask questions after the lecture, then it must have been either so good that no one has anything more to say, or so bad that no one has understood a single word and hence is quiet!

This time, when the questions were being asked, I thought I saw Shanti among the audience. When she saw me looking at her she waved. As always, I was happy to see her. I have known Shanti ever since she was a student in my college. She is one of those people who seem to have boundless energy, always ready to talk and exchange views. She was also very conscious of her social responsibilities, and I know had contributed a portion of her salary to charity from the time she started working.

When the talk came to an end and everyone started dispersing, I waited for Shanti to come up to me. 'Hello Shanti, how are you?' I was expecting her usual chirpy answer. Instead, I was greeted with a low, sad reply. I was taken aback. 'Shanti, what is the matter? Did you fight with your husband? Don't worry. If husband and wife do not fight then they cannot be called a couple. It is part of the deal. Come on cheer up.' I joked to ease her tension.

In the same low tone Shanti said, 'No Madam, that is not the reason.'

'Then is your project deadline approaching and you have not completed it? Shanti, I have always told you that in the software industry the deadline needs to be kept in mind and therefore project management is very essential. I still vaguely remember that you had got highest marks in that. Are you not practising what you learnt in college?'

'That is not the problem. I have completed my project a little bit ahead of time.'

'Then what is worrying you?'

But Shanti did not want to talk there, instead she took me to her cabin. As we walked I noticed many other employees wishing her. By the time we reached her cabin I felt proud that my student was now the boss. The cabin was very well furnished and Shanti closed the blinds before settling down to talk. We each had a cup of coffee and slowly she started confiding in me.

'Madam, I am very unhappy in this job. To an outsider

it might appear that I have the perfect job. I get an excellent salary, my timings are flexible and the office is very close to my house. I do not have to put up with the stress of rush-hour traffic. I am leading a very good team where each person is committed to the work. But my problem is my boss. She is terrible. She has nothing but harsh words for me. I have not heard a single positive remark from her in the three years I have spent here. If I do a good job, she says someone else could have done it in half the time, and heaven help me if something ever goes wrong and things get delayed. She refuses to understand that sometimes things happen which are beyond my control.

'Suppose I am travelling to Bombay, she will deliberately schedule a meeting at ten-thirty in the morning, even though she knows my flight is supposed to land only at ten. With the traffic it is impossible for me to reach the office in half an hour. By the time I reach she would have finished all the important discussions. I work so hard, sometimes staying back the entire night to complete my work before the deadline, but still she says, "you could have been better." Madam it is impossible to satisfy her.'

'Calm down Shanti. Maybe your boss is the kind of person who is never satisfied with anything, that is her nature and you cannot change that. You have to accept her the way she is. You cannot choose your boss.'

'I really don't feel like working with such a person. At times I feel like quitting. With my experience it would not be difficult to get a better job, but I like this company, my team members and the work I am doing. Why should I leave just for the sake of one person?'

'Have you told your higher managers about the situation?'

'I did. But she is the key person in a number of projects and they don't want to lose her.'

'Give it some time. Perhaps slowly she will understand you and the hard work you are putting in.'

Offering her such words of comfort I left the office. When I did not hear from her again after that I assumed Shanti had solved her problem one way or the other. A couple of years passed and one day I was in Jayanagar market, in Bangalore, buying vegetables.

Long back, Jayanagar was a paradise for all middle-class people. But now, staying here has become a very costly affair. The prices of almost everything have shot up and bargaining is strictly looked down upon. The vegetable sellers are so confident of getting their exorbitant prices that they usually refuse to budge even if one ventures to argue.

That day, I was debating heatedly with the shopkeeper who was asking for Rs 10 for one cucumber. I was actually enjoying the skill with which the man was putting forth his arguments. Neither of us was willing to yield even a paisa to the other person.

Suddenly I heard a voice behind me, 'Good evening Madam. How are you?'

It was Shanti, holding a baby by one hand and a basket of fruits and vegetables in another. She had put on a little bit of weight but I instantly saw the old sparkle back in her eyes.

'Hello Shanti! When did you have the baby?' I asked.

'A year ago.'

'You are looking so cheerful, I am very happy for you Shanti.'

'Madam, now I am happy both at home and at work.'

'That is wonderful. How is your boss? Has she changed?'

Shanti took me aside and said, 'She finally got transferred to another office in the city. My new boss is fantastic. Now I really look forward to going to office. If we ever have a disagreement he immediately talks to me and clears the issue. He is always motivating us by appreciating the effort we are putting in. As a result we have performed much better than expected. If we ever have to stay back late into the night, he too stays late. The teamwork and camaraderie is wonderful now. When I was pregnant he kept telling me to take it easy and work from home if I wanted to, but I insisted on going to office till the day before I delivered the baby.'

'This is great news Shanti. It reminds me of the song *"Man vahi, darpan vahi, na jane sab kuch naya naya . . ."*'

'Oh Madam, you are incorrigible.'

Both of us had a hearty laugh standing there in front of the vegetable stall. Then Shanti said, 'Because of our new boss each person is happy working there and feels proud to be part of the team.'

'Yes Shanti, this is something I have learnt over the years—with good attitude you can create a heaven around you, and a good leader can bring about remarkable changes in a team.'

8

The Deserving Candidate

A few years back, I was on a selection committee. We were recruiting people for various posts, most of which had a high remuneration. As a result, there was a lot of pressure on us four committee members.

Overnight, I found my popularity had increased many times over. Forgotten relatives dropped by at my house, friends I had lost touch with appeared out of the blue. Religious heads started telling me how important it was to help people from one's community. Ex-students suddenly remembered when Teachers' Day came and sent me cards. Even in the temple I started getting extra helpings of prasad. I was beginning to enjoy the newfound comforts of life!

Unfortunately for these people all four committee members were very honest and we had decided on the day of our first meeting that we would not entertain any requests. Recruitment would be done based solely on merit.

During one of our interview sessions one day, a young girl walked in. Her name was Nandita and she was good looking, smart and well dressed. We asked our first standard question: why do you think you are suitable for this job? The girl replied, 'I have a great deal of confidence. I can handle the pressures of this job well.'

She was speaking with an American accent, so I asked her where she was from. 'I am from Bangalore,' she replied, 'But most of my relatives stay in the US so I go there during all my holidays.'

'Where have you been in the US? We have many clients there.'

'My uncle Ramakrishnan is a very famous Silicon Valley industrialist. My aunt is a correspondent for *New York Times*. My cousin Rohit works in the White House. So I shuttle between New York, Washington and San Francisco.'

'In our work one is required to interact with different kinds of people often.'

'Oh meeting people and talking to them is not a problem, I enjoy that.'

'Have you any experience of that?'

'Yes. I party a lot and meet lots of people.'

'That is not the same as meeting people on business,' I said and we moved on to the technical questions. She answered adequately well and we finished the interview soon after. As she was leaving, Nandita hesitated near the door. Then she turned and asked, 'Can I ask you something?' I always like it when girls ask questions. For too long the definition of a good girl in our society is one who does not question too much and meekly accepts everything. But I like those who dare to break out of this mould and speak their minds. So I told Nandita to go ahead.

She said, 'The salary you are offering for this job is quite less.' I was taken aback. This was not the kind of question or remark I was expecting. I answered, 'It is very good when you compare it with other companies.'

'Oh it is just enough to pay the rent for an apartment and a driver and cook's salary. I am used to these comforts you see.'

'But you said you live with your parents. The company has a bus and we have an excellent canteen.'

'After I start earning I want to live on my own. That is what everyone does nowadays.' And with these words and a pitiful look at me for my ignorance, she left.

As usual I reached home late that evening. My mother admonished me saying, 'You should have remembered that we have to go to Sharayu's granddaughter's birthday. She has already called thrice. Even if it is late go and say a hello. You have to live in society and can't remain engrossed in your work always.'

Like an obedient child I went to Sharayu's house. The usual kind of party was going on. Men were talking about politics and sports. Women were discussing the next party, and since there was an event manager, the children were busy. It was a hot day and trays of cool drinks were doing the rounds. Suddenly I thought I saw a girl who looked a lot like Nandita. She was wearing a sari and was serving drinks to the guests. When I tried looking at her closely she turned away and avoided my eyes.

I was amazed. I went to Sharayu and asked who the pretty girl serving the drinks was. 'Oh that is Nandita. She is a smart and bright girl. Her father owns a canteen in my husband's office. Our office has sponsored her education. She has completed her engineering recently and is searching for a job. She is a quick learner and adjusts well with everybody. We have invited her to help out today. If you are ever having a party, I would strongly recommend asking her father to do the catering.'

I was speechless.

The interviews carried on for the whole of that week. The last candidate to walk in was a boy in his early twenties. He was ordinarily dressed and seemed to be on the quieter side. His answers were all up to the mark and well thought out. I wanted to know more about him as it is always interesting to talk to bright young minds.

'You answered the questions about computer science very well. Since when have you been interested in the area?' Shyly, he said, 'When I was very young.'

'What age?' I was persistent.

'Probably about eight years.'

'Why so early?'

'My mother is a school teacher and often I was alone at home when she was away at work. The best way to pass the time was to attend some classes.'

Somehow I knew that could not be the only reason. He was obviously very bright and his mother must have spent a lot of time channelising his talents in the right direction. I realized this boy will not boast about his background, but I wanted to know more. 'What about your father? What does he do?'

The boy thought for some time. Then he replied, 'Does it matter? You need only look at my capabilities. If you find me suitable please accept me, or reject me if you don't.'

'How much salary are you expecting?'

The boy said a figure which was higher than what we were offering.

'How do you justify such a high salary for your experience?'

'I will justify it by working hard and taking bottomline responsibility. I will ensure that my work is of the highest standards.'

'Do you mind telling me why you want a higher salary?'

'I want to donate a part of it to a trust which helps bright students continue their education if they can't pay the fees.'

I was touched by his answer. After this there was nothing more to ask. When the boy left we were unanimous that we wanted to take him. As we were talking, the clerk who was handing out the travel allowance to those who had come from out of town for the interview, walked in. He said, 'Could you sign for the last candidate? He did not claim his allowance. He said he stayed with his aunt and came to town on some personal work too.'

Now I was amazed at the boy's honesty. I looked closely at his form and at the permanent address. He was the son of a very successful doctor. Obviously money or fame had not robbed him of his honesty and simplicity.

9

The Business of Philanthropy

Sri Hiralal Jain was a successful pharmacist and businessman. He was kind-hearted, unassuming and shy. He had started his career in a pharmaceutical company and had gone on to build his own empire through hard work and honesty.

One day, he came to meet me. We talked about our various projects and initiatives for some time, then he started talking about himself. 'Mrs Murty, God has been exceedingly kind to me. My company is doing well and we are able to launch new products regularly. As a result we have a large range. I have only one son who is studying abroad. I am sure he will complete his studies, join my work and make it even more successful. I am always busy with work and travel and now I feel I have made enough money to last another generation. But there is one gap. I feel I have not done enough to give back to society in any big way. That is why I have come here today with a request.'

I was still not sure where the conversation was leading, and asked him to go on.

'I have learnt a lot about your work with the Infosys Foundation. You help people in the villages and slums. So I want to give you some basic medicines that you can distribute to the poor people. You can appoint a doctor to help you with your work in slums, I will pay his salary and also provide the medicines free.'

I was touched. I said, 'Your proposal is wonderful but we already have some doctors who work part-time on our projects. I will talk to them and tell them to make a list of the medicines they require. I will send you that list every month and come and collect the medicines at an appointed time from your office.'

'No, no, you need not come. I will send them to you. But I have one condition.'

I was worried. I should have known. No one gives a free lunch!

Hiralal Jain said, 'Nobody must come to know of my association with this work. I don't want my name or my company's name to appear anywhere. I want to savour the joy of giving without the publicity. I will remain an unknown donor.'

This was a most unusual request. Normally, most of the people who come with donations are already planning their media statements. They may give the smallest sums of money, but hearing them talk it would seem that they had funded our entire operations.

I agreed readily to his proposal. And so it was decided that every month his head clerk Karim would come with a box of the required medicines. His delivery van came near our office to some retail outlets and our supply would come in that.

I thanked Hiralal Jain and sent up a prayer that 'May his tribe increase'.

So the system fell into place. Initially Hiralal donated Rs 10,000 worth of medicines, which slowly went up to Rs 50,000. He gave us his old Fiat car so the doctors could visit the slums in ease. But we hardly met. Whenever I called him to thank him he would tell me not to waste my time. When I sent him pictures of our medical camps he would call me and say he did not require proof of our work. He had faith in us.

Years went by. Our work got more and more attention and many people started coming up and offering help. One pharmacy store offered to give us as much medicines we wanted every month. But I was reluctant to close the relationship with Hiralal Jain.

One morning I got the news that he had passed away in his sleep. I prayed in silence. A pious soul like that had to go with minimum of fuss and suffering. I went to his office to pay my last respects. Ironically, I realized it was my first visit to his office in so many years. It was simple and decorated spartanly. I noticed a young handsome man in white with red, swollen eyes. The head clerk Karim whispered to me, 'That is Saket Saab. He has just returned from the US.'

I gathered Saket had studied for his MBA in the US and was working there for some years. Now he would come back and take over the business.

Days passed and for two months the old system with Hiralal's company continued. The medicine parcels reached us on time. The third month there was no sign of it. I thought I would wait for a few days and then call. When there was still no sign I dialled Hiralal's office number. A polite voice answered from the other side. I assumed it was the receptionist and wondered what had happened to Karim. I was made to hold the line for some time. Then finally I was told, 'Saket would like to meet you at his office tomorrow morning at nine.'

Since he was the donor it was my duty to respect his wishes. I reached at 8.45 and was taken aback at the changes. Gone was the old spartan look. This was a modern corporate house with a pretty receptionist, fresh flowers in vases, framed paintings on the walls. There was a leather sofa set and the floor was now gleaming granite. A young lady ushered me to an antechamber and offered me some drinks. There was a huge portrait of Hiralal Jain in the hallway. Soon it was nearing nine o'clock, and I started making my way to Saket's office. But I was stopped by the receptionist. 'I am sorry, Saket sir is talking to a business executive and this may take ten more minutes. Please wait.' So I waited. When it was 9.45, I decided it was enough and told her I was leaving. She spoke on the intercom and showed me in finally. When I entered I saw the business executive was still there. Saket looked at him apologetically and excused himself for five minutes. Then he turned to me and came straight to the point.

'I have been going through our old records. My father gave you enormous amounts of money anonymously. I think that was a mistake and a waste of money. I am willing to continue our association but on some new terms. Our company's and my name should appear prominently whenever you hold a camp. You must send someone to pick up the medicines every month. I can give you supplies only from our surplus stock and not what you want. You must address our employees once a year and talk about our donation. After all, philanthropy is key to business promotion.'

By this time, five minutes were over and I got up. Politely I said, 'Thank you but I cannot agree. I cannot find surplus diseases to suit your surplus medicines. I wanted to thank you for the support your father gave us over the years. The conditions were of his choice and we respected that. Now that our association is ending I just want to say, don't mix business and philanthropy. You will not be able to do justice to either. Your father understood that. Perhaps one day you will too.'

I left the office and in the hallway stood and looked at Hiralal Jain's photo for a minute. Silently I said a final goodbye and stepped out.

10

A HELPING HAND

Like many natural disasters of great magnitude, the tsunami waves that struck the shores of our country in December 2004, opened our eyes to the myriad shades of human nature. Through the media, we saw and heard time and again about the devastation wreaked on coastal communities and how aid was pouring in from everywhere. In places which were in the news, the victims were soon inundated by a wave of relief material—saris, dhotis, towels, bed sheets, cooking stoves, vessels, plastic buckets, drinking water, mats, etc. In towns like Nagapattinam, Kadalur, Velankani and Karaikal, one could also see heaps of old and worn-out clothes which no one wanted, lying untouched on either sides of the road.

The relief camps and wedding halls in these places had plenty of volunteers initially, distributing food or ration, giving injections to stop the spread of diseases and helping the injured. Often the victims expressed their dissatisfaction at the food being served as local food habits were being overlooked. Instead they demanded to be allowed to cook their own food. The donor and the benefactor were right in their own ways in this matter.

Our team from the foundation set out first on a fact-finding mission before starting the relief work. For one, we decided to visit the towns in the news later, after they had moved away from the airwaves and the first rush of volunteers had departed. Meanwhile, we went to the smaller, lesser known villages and made a list of the essential articles needed by the people. We discovered that in some towns there was plenty of relief material, but the people had no place to store them and incidents of theft or fights over ownership were becoming common. In other places we realized that the most basic material required for the people to get their lives back together were missing.

Armed with this data we devised the 'tsunami survival kit'. It was a bit like the survival kits I had seen in some stores in the USA, though those were meant for mountaineering accidents. We made some modifications and started assembling our own kit: a huge aluminium trunk with a five-level lock and twenty-five articles that we found were essential for the survivors. While the trunk itself could be used for storage, inside we included things like a tarpaulin, medicines, torch, a small radio, groceries, toiletries, etc. It was a novel idea and our team worked tirelessly in gathering everything.

We purchased most of the items from the source, and the moment the suppliers heard it was for relief work they offered us large discounts and even delivered the material free.

Given the scale of our work, we needed a large area to spread out all the items, assemble the kits and to check if we had put in everything in all the trunks. There were ten of us working on this. My student George Joseph offered us the use of the huge basement of his bungalow, somewhere in the outskirts of Bangalore. We got all the material delivered straight to the basement and started our work in earnest. I was amazed at my team's dedication and professionalism. They assembled nearly a thousand trunks in two days. George too visited us often to ask if we needed anything and made provisions for snacks and tea. The whole process was going smoothly and soon we were ready to start loading the trunks on to the trucks. Now we had a problem. It was difficult to do the loading from our basement workplace and we felt it would be better if we could store them together in a place accessible to a truck. George, as usual, had a solution to our problem. 'Don't worry,' he told me. 'The adjacent plot is empty and I know the owner. The architect comes there once in a while, but if we take permission from his office I am sure they will not have a problem with us storing the trunks there for one night. Nobody will say no to such work.'

The plot was big and a corner one and therefore most convenient for loading the material. We all thought it was a good idea.

The next day, a bright young lady arrived at our basement. Beaming, she introduced herself as a junior architect in the architect's office. 'Lankesh, our main architect is out of station. I came to know through George that you would like to store the trunks on this site. I think it is a nice idea. Not all of us are able to go and help the victims but this way we can do our small bit for them.'

'Thank you. But I hope it will not hinder your work!' I replied.

'No Madam, not at all. Anyway the survey people are coming next week. Please do not hesitate to ask us for any help.'

By the time our work was completed and we shifted everything to the neighbouring plot, it was almost evening. The truck was supposed to come the next morning and all our volunteers were just waiting to go home and rest. They had worked very hard and I felt proud of them. I have learnt that it is better to have ten people who work sincerely than to have hundred people working halfheartedly. I was lucky that all my team members were so hardworking.

Just as we were about to leave a Mercedes drew up in front of us and a man emerged from it, prominently bearing his cellphone and blackberry. He looked smart and was well dressed, but the expression on his face clearly showed his displeasure over some matter.

He approached me and without a word of greeting demanded, 'Who gave you the permission to store your stuff on this plot?'

I realized this was Lankesh, the main architect.

As politely as I could, I answered, 'George told me that he would talk to you and take permission from your office. Yesterday your assistant came and said it was all right. So, I assumed that you were aware of it.'

'No. That is not true. I was travelling and nobody has informed me about this. You may be doing relief work but please understand that you have put your material here without my permission. You should have taken my permission and not my assistant's. I am the architect, and this entire area is my responsibility.'

Surprised at his outburst I said, 'I am sorry for the mistake. Anyway it is a matter of another ten hours. Tomorrow morning the trucks will come and we will load everything on to them.'

'It does not concern me whether it is a matter of a night or a day. I had called the survey people to do their job today. They will come any time. I want you to remove everything.'

'Your assistant told me that they will come only next week. How can I possibly remove so many heavy trunks in such a short time and where can we keep them?' I pleaded.

'I do not know. It is not my problem. Perhaps you can pile them on the roadside. You have not taken my permission. If you had told me earlier, I would have made some space for you.' The man would not budge from his position.

By this time I realized that it was not a matter of us taking permission. He only wanted to show off his power to us. I have met many such people in my work and I knew the futility of arguing with him. But my team members were all young and, by now, boiling over with anger at the man's impudence. They started arguing with him but I stopped them.

'Sorry. I will shift these trunks right now and keep them on the road. We will vacate your plot at the earliest. It means a lot of extra work for us but that is the penalty we will have to pay for incurring your displeasure.'

'Ma'am, if you keep the trunks on the roadside, they

may be stolen or somebody may raise further objections,' Kumar, one of the volunteers, raised his voice in panic.

I smiled and said, 'Don't worry. We will put our banner there and no thief will touch the material. I am sure none of the other neighbours will complain when they know for whom they are meant.'

And it happened just like that. The trunks were kept on the roadside that night and loaded on to the truck the next morning without a hitch. After the trucks left, Kumar came to my office. He was looking dejected and for a while sat with a thoughtful look on his face. Then he said, 'Ma'am, we don't know the victims, they are not related to us in any way. Some of us don't even speak their language. We are doing this only because we want to help in some way. Why can't people understand this? The architect was so rude to you yesterday. Did you not get perturbed? You said you meet people like him often in your work. Tell me Ma'am, why should we do this work if we don't get anything in return except harsh words?'

Just then there was a knock on my door and the security guard I had seen on the plot where we had initially kept the trunks came into the room. I was taken aback and wondered why he had come to my office now that the whole episode was over.

He said, 'Madam, what Lankesh sir did yesterday was wrong. But I am only a poor employee, I could not stand up to him then. After you left yesterday I finished my duty and spent the night guarding the trunks. I did not take your permission for that but I had seen the care with which you had assembled them and how tirelessly you had worked. I too want to do my bit for the people. I don't have much savings so I wanted to give you my one day's salary. Please use it however you think is best.' With these words, he handed me a soiled and sealed envelope and took his leave. I opened it and out dropped a cheque for Rs 160.

I looked at it for some time, then I turned to Kumar and said, 'This cheque is worth Rs 16 lakh to me. You asked why we should continue working? It is for people like these, who open their hearts and put their faith in us.'

Working in a disaster relief area opens ones eyes not only to the suffering of the people affected, but also brings out the true character in many people. When the tsunami hit our shores, while most people responded with bravery and generosity, there were plenty of stories of people using it as a publicity gimmick to further their own agendas.

Soon after the rehabilitation work started, it was clear that a massive amount of money was required. Funds started pouring in and almost everyone was seen to be busy with fundraising. Among them happened to be my friend Rekha. Now Rekha is a good person, but talking to her for too long gives me a headache because she refuses to ever come to the point. She lives alone in Bangalore as her husband is in Dubai and daughter is settled in Delhi. She has a lot of energy and often does not know what to do with it!

One day, when I was busy supervising our tsunami relief work in Bangalore, she landed up in my office and started chatting about the effects of the waves. The description carried on for some time, till I got tired and said, 'Yes Rekha I know. I have just spent a few weeks in these areas and have seen for myself the extent of devastation. Did you have some work with me? I am busy with coordinating our relief programme.'

Then she came to the point.

'You know, in the area where I live, there is a youth club. The boys and girls from that club went from door to door collecting money for the victims. They are very keen to hand over the money to you. Will you come and accept it? It would encourage them to do more such work.'

I was happy to hear about this and agreed to go there. After all youngsters need to be appreciated when they take initiative and do such work. But Rekha was still sitting looking hesitant. Finally she said, 'Sudha, the children have ended up spending money from their pockets, going all over the area on their bikes and mopeds . . .'

Immediately I replied, 'In that case Rekha, tell them to deduct that expenditure from the collection before handing it over to me.' Rekha left my office looking happy.

I reached the locality on the appointed day. I was astonished to see that elaborate arrangements had been made for a full-fledged function. There was a well-decorated dais and marquee. A sound system was in place and even the media had been invited. Coffee and biscuits were being served from a table placed in one corner of the field. Soon the function started. There were plenty of people willing to talk and for a long time each person spoke about the tsunami, the devastation, why it had happened etc. People who had never visited the areas tried to speak knowledgeably about the plight of the victims.

Finally, Rekha, who was moderating, handed over a beautifully decorated purse to me. A gang of young people came onto the dais and proceeded to garland me. A mike was thrust at me and I spoke a few words of appreciation and encouragement. Finally it was over and I made my way back to my car. Already, in my mind, I was planning the things I could buy with the contribution. Some milk powder, tarpaulin or fishing nets? I thought it was wonderful how they had collected so much money and handed it over to me out of sheer trust. With such thoughts still on my mind, I opened the purse.

Two pages fell out first. I looked closely and realized it was the expenditure list. There were amounts marked against marquee, video and photo coverage, sound system, flowers, decoration, taxi hire etc. They had collected Rs 10,295 and had spent Rs 10,285. A brand new ten-rupee note fell into my hands from between the pages. That was their final contribution to the relief work!

The next morning there was a photo in the paper of a beaming Rekha handing over the purse to me. I looked at it and added Rs 10 against her name in our list of contributors!

***

It is of course not always true that the donors work with their own agendas. Sometimes the beneficiaries too pose problems.

When disaster strikes an area, I have seen that often the actual population of that area almost doubles. Beggars and other people from the surrounding and even far-off places start pouring in, hoping to win some easy bread by joining the refugee camps and standing in the ration queues. When the relief agencies don't coordinate their material well, they end up giving away surplus material to the victims, who then sell it to others. In fact, I have come to realize that our country does not lack relief agencies and donors. What we lack is an efficient system of disbursal.

So at the foundation, we have devised a system. When we take up any relief work, we first do a survey of the area, talk to people and study the depth and nature of the damage. Then we go with only the material that is essential. Before we start disbursing that we make a list of all the people in the area and hand out coupons. The material is handed over when they present the coupons to us at the camp. This way we are sure that the aid reaches the right people and bogus 'victims' cannot take advantage. The system is tedious and time-consuming but we are assured that we are helping the right people.

During our tsunami relief work, we went once to a village where we initially had a meeting with the villagers to discuss their requirements. The next day we came with our material and the queue started forming. Soon we realized we had a problem on our hands. Many people were demanding extra materials and some others were returning time and again for further helpings. We had taken about 15 per cent more than the amount our list indicated but at this rate we would have needed 100 per cent extra.

While I was trying to talk to some people and tell them that things were going wrong, a middle-aged man spoke up from the crowd. 'Yes there are some extra people here today. They too need these things. You are not doing us a favour by giving us all this. They were given to you by other people to hand over to us. It is all ours anyway. And you people come here only because you want some fame saying you have done work. You are doing this for your selfish reasons. Getting all this material is our right and we shall decide how much we want, not you. If you cannot give us, go away. We won't accept anything.'

Many volunteers were very upset to hear this. Some had taken leave without pay to stay in these areas and do the work because they wanted to help. Arguments began and voices started getting raised. But with age I have learnt patience and realized something had to be done before a full-fledged fight broke out.

As calmly as possible I said, 'When we came to your village yesterday you said there are 200 families here. Each one wrote the family's name and number of members. You agreed yesterday that you needed material only for these 200 families. To be on the safer side we have got enough for 230 families. Now you are saying people have come from outside and they too should be given a share. This is a disaster area. We are not entertaining guests and relatives. You have to survive. We cannot do magic and create extra material. If you feel we are helping you out of selfishness, is it not better that we are selfish in this manner rather than hoarding things for ourselves? Please don't try to threaten us. Remember if someone is helping you today, you can be grateful and help someone else in need another time. Today people are queuing up to help you, but after a month the world will forget. If you burn your bridges now you will pay a heavy price. Your behaviour today will determine how the world behaves towards you later.'

The man had no answer. He bowed his head in shame.

At the end of each semester, when the coursework is complete, I do not allow my students to sit and study in the library. Instead, every few days I arrange a debate in the classroom on some topic, where each person has to say something. I do this in order to hone their communication, especially verbal, skills. We all look forward to these debates, which sometimes become so strong and emotional that I have to jump into the fray and remind everyone that it is merely a classroom discussion.

Once, the subject was marriage. The students were discussing various issues that arise during a wedding, like the expenses incurred for the ceremony, the advantages and disadvantages of arranged marriages, how well the two people need to know one another before taking the step, and so on. Some of them said, 'A wedding has always been looked upon as a social occasion in our country. If the families can afford it, why shouldn't they spend as much money as they desire on the preparations and meet other people.' Others said, 'The amount of money spent at a wedding has become a status symbol. It has become a place for exchanging gossip. Parents end up spending their life savings in these ceremonies.' One of them, Sunitha, elaborated further, 'In our country, most bonded labourers have got into a debt trap because of high marriage expenditures. These lavish weddings should be banned.'

I stepped in at this point and told them gently that the expense and the ceremonies don't determine the success of the marriage. Rather, it is the understanding that needs to develop between husband and wife. To prove this, I told them the story of the most successful marriage I have seen so far in my life—that of Yellamma and Madha.

I met them when I happened to be spending a night at a tiny village in the course of my work. I had had a wonderful meal and was enjoying an after-dinner stroll around the village. It was a full-moon night and the quiet and serenity were most welcome to my ears: no noises of phones ringing, cars honking, aeroplanes roaring overhead. Instead leaves on the trees were rustling gently in the breeze, a bird or a dog was calling out now and then into the dark night, which was lit only by the moonlight. Gowramma, the local lady accompanying me, was talking as she walked with me, describing the village's problems of drinking water, procuring pesticides and lack of medical facilities. We were walking towards the large banyan tree, the heart of the village, when I heard someone singing a folk song. I was struck by the beauty and soulfulness of the rendition and asked Gowramma about the singer. She said it must be Madha singing for his wife Yellamma. I immediately asked if I could visit them and we walked to their hut.

Madha and Yellamma were perhaps the poorest people in that village. They had to beg for their meals every day. Yellamma was quite sick and when I reached their hut, she was lying down, while Madha was massaging her feet and singing. It was a rare but touching sight. We started chatting with them, and I asked candidly, 'What problems do you face in this village?'

Yellamma replied, 'We don't have any problems. We do everything together, dividing the work between us. We usually ask each other's opinion. We always tell what is on our minds and if one is wrong the other does not hesitate to correct. If I cannot go out, Madha fetches alms for both of us. We believe that in this journey of life, we should be together in everything. Whether it is some special alms or only a pot of water, we share whatever we earn. We spend the day begging in different parts of the village but are always glad to be with each other at night. We trust each other and are happy with our lives, full of hardships though it is.'

Standing there in front of their ramshackle hut under the bright moonlight, I realized I was listening to great words of wisdom. Yellamma and Madha were the poorest of the poor, uneducated, and had faced great adversities in life, but they had learnt the most valuable lesson: how to live happily with one's partner.

In our society now, marriage is often treated as a security measure, and wedding ceremonies as social events where the status of the couple is on display. It is rare to come across a couple who understand that they are on a journey together, sharing their joys and sorrows. For

Yellamma and Madha marriage was a partnership, not a burden or an object to be flaunted.

THE GRATEFUL TENANT

It was a Sunday morning and for once I was eager to attend a function. It is not something I normally look forward to, but this one was special; it was the housewarming ceremony of my friends Ramesh and Sheela's new house.

Ramesh is a professor and Sheela works in a bank. They earn well enough but most of it goes in looking after their large family. In fact, I knew Ramesh had had to spend a large amount on his sister's wedding a few years back. Given this situation, and the fact that with land prices shooting up in Bangalore, it has become difficult for an honest salaried person to buy a house, I knew my friends were very proud and happy to have been able to do so. I too was keen to meet them and be a part of their happiness.

The house was at a new layout in the outskirts of Bangalore. It was simply built and just right for a family of their size. I could see the satisfaction on Ramesh and Sheela's faces. Many of our old friends had also come and we spent a lot of time chatting. We had lunch together and time seemed to fly, there was no time to feel tired or bored. Right after finishing lunch, we were sitting on some chairs laid out in the shade outside the house, and waiting for the paan to arrive. Someone had gone to the nearest market to get it and we knew it would take a while for him to return. We were talking of this and that and I was looking at the house, when I noticed a plaque attached next to the gate. It had the name of the house, Shyamkamal, engraved on polished black granite.

In my experience, people name their houses after their own or children's names. Or it is named after the family deity, like Venkateshwara Nilaya or Raghavendra Prasad or Beereshwara Krupa, etc. Of late more exotic names like Love Nest, Paradise, Seventh Heaven and Sukha Villa, Aishwarya Villa, etc. have been added to the list. (Of course here 'villa' is the French word for 'house' and not the Kannada word meaning 'no'!) Some people with an artistic or literary bent of mind name their houses Megha Dhoot, Nadaswara, Varshini, etc.

But Shyamkamal was not fitting into any of these categories. So I asked, 'Sheela, why is your house called Shyamkamal? I have only heard of the movie *Neelkamal*!'

Sheela and Ramesh exchanged a look. Ramesh said, 'It is a combination of the names of the two people who changed our lives, and the ones we remember and thank each day.'

'What do you mean by that? Who are they?' I asked.

I had known Ramesh and Sheela for many years. His father Madappa was from a village near Dharwad in north Karnataka and Sheela's family was distantly related to Ramesh's. We had been friends from childhood and would go to school and play together. We often ate our meals

together and knew each other's relatives quite well. I was
quite sure I had never heard of or met anyone called
Shyama-Kamal among their relatives.

Ramesh explained, 'Shyamkamal stands for Shyama
Rao and Kamala. Do you remember when I was in college
in Dharwad, I used to stay with an old couple?'

I thought back to those days of long ago. Of course I
remembered. With age, I have discovered it is easier to
remember the events of the distant past rather than what
happened earlier in the day. In Dharwad, there was an
old couple who used to rent their outhouse to college
students. Ramesh must have stayed there for six years.
But I was still puzzled. Why would he want to name his
house after the couple who were after all only his
landlords. Ramesh noticed the mystified look on my face,
and explained, 'You may not know, Sudha, but those days
my family was much against my going to Dharwad for
higher studies. They wanted me to stay back in the village
and look after the fields. At that time, Shyama Rao
supported me wholeheartedly in my decision to study in a
bigger town. He was a retired postmaster and my father's
friend, and he convinced my father to send me to
Dharwad with promises of looking after me. He became
more important than my father to me. He gave me a place
to stay. My meals used to come from my village in the
state government bus every day, but if ever the bus did
not come, or I could not go to the bus stand for some
reason, his wife, Kamala Bai would share their meal with
me. She did not let me go hungry for a single day. And
you know how hard up we were, so if I got late in

depositing my college fees, Shyama Rao would put aside some money from his meagre pension and help me out.'

'But you used to run errands for them and do odd jobs around their house. In fact we used to call you their Man Friday behind your back,' said Raghav, Ramesh's roommate.

'I won't agree with you Raghav. Think of the old couple. They had no need to do all those things for me. They were not rich but they went out of their way to help me out of my difficulties. Without their help, I do not know where and what I would have been today. I will never forget their generosity. Even after I finished college and was unemployed and despairing, I remember Shyama Rao would speak encouraging words to me and lift my spirits. "Don't feel bad. So what if you have lost the battle, you will win the war", is something he told me often.'

'But why did you name this house after them?' I went back to my first question.

'It was my father's suggestion. You see, he brought me up, his son, because it was his duty, the way I am doing everything possible to bring up my children. But there are some people who do things out of affection, and not duty, and they change your life with their love and generosity. My father said this house should be named after the people who played such an important part in my education. This is a story that my children need to know. I also want them to understand the gratitude I feel towards Shyama Rao and Kamala Bai not through mere words but by my actions.'

Ramesh and his father's gesture moved me immensely.

They reminded me of Dr BR Ambedkar, who decided to call himself Ambedkar after his teacher. It is people like them who reaffirm our faith in humanity and the culture of this ancient country.

14

A Foreigner, Always

Gautam Buddha was born 2,500 years ago as Prince Siddharth in Lumbini, in present-day Nepal. Throughout his lifetime he crisscrossed the subcontinent spreading his message of peace, tolerance and the righteous path. Shravasthi, Rajagraha, Sarnath, Boddh Gaya, Kushinagar are some of the places he visited and which became important centres of Buddhism. Though he imparted most of his teachings in India, in the ensuing centuries, Buddhism spread all over the world. Today, Sri Lanka, Japan, Korea, Thailand are some countries where Buddhism is flourishing. And in the Indian subcontinent too, there are places which retain strong links with Buddhist history.

Nearly twenty-five kilometers from Islamabad, there is a sleepy town called Takshila. At one time, it was the site of the world's oldest university, and an important centre of Buddhist learning. King Ashoka, the great patron of Buddhism, built many viharas here where scholars discussed philosophy and religion for centuries. Hiuen Tsang described the glory and beauty of Takshila in his writings.

Now, all that remains of that bustling university are

the ruins. The Pakistan government has converted part of it into a museum, where one can see splendid works of art including heads of Buddha statues which have been excavated, jewels and panels depicting the life of Buddha. For anyone interested in Buddhism and its history, this museum is a place that has to be seen.

Recently I visited Pakistan for the first time. Though I was there on some other work, I had decided long back that if ever I got the chance to visit Pakistan, I would go to Takshila. I landed in Islamabad with many of the usual preconceived notions about the country in my mind. But soon I saw that women were moving about freely and not always in burqas! The sumptuous meal of channa bhatura, alu paratha and jalebi that our host had prepared for us made us feel more at home. I spent some time shopping for clothes and again, the bazaars and shops were not too different from ours, and we ended up buying the latest bargains. Our taxi driver was humming what turned out to be the latest Hindi film number when I heard him closely. And like in our country, there was a delay in the flight I was to take. So it was not surprising that I found myself feeling quite comfortable.

The next day, I set off for Takshila with a French group. We got a bit delayed in reaching the museum and the curator, perhaps guessing our keen desire to see the exhibits said, 'It is nearing closing time. Why don't you all go in and start looking around, I will explain everything. Your tour organizer can get your tickets meanwhile from the counter.' This seemed like a good idea to all of us and we were soon absorbed in looking at the wonderful articles on display. For me it was additionally moving as I was fulfilling a long-cherished desire. I was seeing parts of our history which I had only read about in books come alive. After a detailed tour, the curator led us outside. There, for the first time, I noticed the ticket window. The rates were Rs 200 for foreigners and Rs 25 for locals. When the organizer handed me my ticket counterfoil I realized I was holding one for Rs 200. Thinking there had been some mistake I went up to the man at the ticket window. 'I understand your reasons for charging more from foreigners as you need all the funds you can get for the upkeep of the museum,' I said. 'But why are you charging me Rs 200? I am from India. This place is as much a part of my heritage as yours.'

The man looked unmoved. In a firm voice he replied, 'You are an Indian and therefore a foreigner.'

The words struck me deeply. I realized, in spite of the similarities in our dress, language, food and even love for Bollywood movies, Partition had divided us forever. It had made us strangers in each other's lands and even in a place like that ancient university town, the Buddha's words of love and tolerance were not enough to bring us together. The Rs 200 ticket brought me crashing back to reality!

15

THE LINE OF SEPARATION

During my trip to Pakistan, I was part of a large group. Each person in the group was keen to visit one place or the other in that country. Some wanted to see Takshila, others Lahore, Islamabad or Karachi. One day, we were having a discussion about this and everyone was voicing his opinion loudly. I noticed only Mrs Roopa Kapoor was sitting quietly. She was a seventy-five-year-old lady from Chennai and did not speak much unless spoken to. So I asked if there was any place she wanted to visit.

Without any hesitation, she said, 'I have to visit Pindi.'

'Where is Pindi? Is it some small town or village? I don't think we will have the time to make a detour like that from our packed itinerary.' Roopa smiled at my ignorance and said, 'I meant Rawalpindi. It is called Pindi for short by those who stay there.' I was intrigued. 'How do you know? Have you ever stayed there?'

'I was born and brought up there,' she replied, and then slowly she told me the story of her life.

She had stayed in Rawalpindi till the age of nineteen, when she got married and settled down in Chennai. Now Chennai was her home and she could speak Tamil and make excellent Tamil dishes like puliyogare and rasam, as well as any natural-born Tamilian. But she had always yearned to come back and see her childhood home if she ever got the chance.

Soon we reached Islamabad and I was surprised to find it surrounded by mountains, as cool as a hill station. Roopa saw my surprise and said, 'Islamabad is a new city. Rawalpindi is a sister city, but it is older. Islamabad was built after the Partition with wide roads, shopping centres and rose gardens. Pindi is only twenty odd kilometers away from Islamabad.' By now the soft-spoken, introverted Mrs Kapoor had become quite garrulous. There was a spark in her eyes and she spoke non-stop. Many of us wanted to see Islamabad first, but she insisted on going on to Rawalpindi.

She needed a companion for the trip and I volunteered to go with her. She was now quite excited, and told me, 'I want to see the house I left fifty-seven years ago.'

'That's a good idea,' I said. Then I remembered the lovely bouquet of flowers I had been presented on landing at Islamabad which I was still carrying. 'I will present this to whoever is staying in your house now.'

She was touched.

As the car left Islamabad airport behind, Mrs Kapoor started pointing out the sights to me like a tour guide. She showed an old building on the left side of the road in a crowded area and said, 'That used to be an electrical goods manufacturing factory. Its owner Kewal Ram Sahani was my father's friend. My friends and I would come to this house for Lakshmi pooja during Diwali.'

I told the driver to slow down a little so that she could

cherish the journey. The car passed Sadar Bazar and looking at an old building with many shops, she said, 'Here my father's cousin Ratan Sethi owned a jewellery shop along with his partner Maqbool Khan. It was known as Khan and Sethi. My wedding jewellery was made here.'

She continued pointing out various buildings, each holding some fond memory for her. But many a times the buildings she was looking for had changed to new skyscrapers and she got disoriented. Suddenly the car stopped. A tyre was punctured, and the driver said it would take him a while to fix it. Roopa Kapoor was restless. She did not want to wait even a minute more than required. So she said, 'You change the tyre. In the meantime I will go and visit some of the old places. We will join you in the next main road. To go to the main road, you take a left turn and the first right turn. You wait for us there.'

She behaved as if she knew every inch of that area and I followed her quietly. We walked into a small lane. She explained, 'I have been here many times with my friends Fatima and Noor. This used to be known as Tailor's Road. My neighbour Mehboob Khan's wife Mehrunnisa Chachi was an expert in designing new embroidery patterns. We used to come and give the designs. Come we will take a short cut . . . that is where my uncle lived.'

By now she was talking more to herself and making her way with ease through the narrow lanes. We went to the next road. There were old houses on the road and she went into the first huge bungalow. She said, 'This was my uncle Motiram Rai's house and the next house was that of Allah Baksh. They were great friends and loved each other. I still remember whenever Allah Baksh Chacha planted a tree in his house, my uncle would plant the same. This mango tree here was planted on a Basant Panchami day. There was so much of joy in both houses. My grandmother prepared kheer and sent me to Allah Baksh's house with a jug full of it. While I was carrying that jug, I bumped into a young man and the hot kheer fell on his feet. I was so scared and embarrassed.'

'Did you know him?'

'Not then but later. I married him!'

She then looked up at the tree and said, 'This has become so old now.'

We walked in through the gate. There was no one around and I was afraid we would be stopped by someone for trespassing. But Roopa was least bothered. It was as if she was in a world of her own. She walked to the back yard while I stood hesitating in the front. A couple walked in and were visibly surprised to see a stranger standing in their garden, that too in a sari. It was also just then that I noticed a board hanging in front of the door. It said 'Dr Salim and Dr Salma: Dentist'.

I started apologizing and explained about Roopa to them. Their faces lost the look of suspicion as soon as I finished my story. Roopa was meanwhile still looking at all the trees and remembering her childhood. The couple welcomed us in courteously. 'Please sit down. Do join us for a cup of tea.' They pulled up two chairs.

By now I was feeling very awkward, disturbing them

in the morning. But Dr Salim said, 'Please sit. We are glad you came. Our grandparents too were from Surat in Gujarat. They emigrated to Pakistan and I was born and brought up here. My parents talk with great nostagia about Surati farsan, parsi dhansak and khakra.'

Just to make conversation I said, 'It must be difficult maintaining such a large bungalow now.'

Dr Salim replied, 'We moved to this house some years back. You see this house happens to resemble the one my parents lived in in Surat, and they made me promise that I would not break it and make apartments as long as I stayed here. Allah has been kind to us and we don't need the money. Our neighbour Allah Baksh's children sold their property long back and now there is a commercial complex.'

By then Roopa had finished wandering in the garden and I formally introduced her to the couple. She asked if she could see the house from the inside. Dr Salim agreed happily. 'After we purchased this house ten years ago we made very few modifications. It is perhaps in the same state as you last saw it,' he said.

I walked in with Roopa. She looked into the main room and said, 'This was where my grandfather used to sit and control the house.' Then she pointed out a coloured glass door and said Allah Baksh's wife had painted it for them. 'That was the window through which she would send dry fruits to my aunt', 'That was where we used to fly kites.' Every brick, every wall held a memory for her. Finally I reminded her that it was time we left. We walked back to the garden and said our goodbyes to the couple. Dr

Salim handed us a packet. 'There is no time for you to eat, but I cannot send two elders away without offering anything. Please take this and if god is willing we will meet again.'

We came out of the house and when we reached the main road the car was there, having followed Roopa's directions. Now she wanted to see her own house.

She told the driver, 'Take a right turn from the Chauraha. I know the way. The first building on the right side is Al-Ameen School for girls and a little further there is a Jesus and Mary convent. A little ahead on the left side, there is a government boys' school. Next to that is the Idgah maidan. Next to that is a lane with five huge bungalows. Each plot is an acre in size. The first one belonged to Kewal Ram. Second to Mia Mehboob Khan and the third one to Sardar Supreet Singh. Fourth one to Rai saheb and the fifth was ours . . .'

She talked on and the driver followed her directions. She was mostly right. Yes the red brick building on the right was Al-Ameen School for girls. The Jesus and Mary convent was now a Loyola College and the government boys' school had become a degree college. But the Idgah maidan was not there. Instead there was a shopping complex. The five beautiful bungalows she described were also missing. Instead there was a mass of shops, hotels, video libraries piled next to each other. Roopa became upset.

'Madam, are you sure it is the same road?', the driver asked politely.

'Of course I am sure. I was born here. I spent nineteen

years here. You were not even born then. How can I make a mistake?'

She told him to stop the car and got off to search. She was sure the house was still there behind the new buildings. She was possessed, as if searching for a lost child, or a precious jewel.

'My house was yellow in colour and there were two storeys. It had an entrance from the right side. From my house I could see the Idgah maidan. Two years back a friend of mine who also stayed here came to see the place and she told me the house was still very much here.'

She turned to me and continued, 'You know, once I had unknowingly walked on the wet cement floor near the entrance of the house and my footmark stayed there forever. My father wanted to keep it as a reminder of me after I got married and went away. I can recognize my house without any trouble.' But there was no house of that description in that area, with the footmark in the entrance. I knew by this time that the house was not there. But Roopa was reluctant to accept it.

We stood in front of the building where she said her house used to be. It was a hotel and a chowkidar was sitting at the entrance.

I asked him, 'How old is this hotel?'

He got up and replied, 'It is only a year old.'

'How long have you been working here?'

'Ever since the old building was demolished and the construction started.'

Roopa was quiet now.

'Was there a two-storeyed yellow building here with

the entrance on the right and footprints along the portico?'

'Yes. There was a building like that but I don't remember the footprints.'

Now I knew that Roopa's house had been demolished to make way for this hotel. I looked at the chowkidar and told him, 'That was my friend's house.'

'Oh please come inside. So what if your house is not there? The hotel stands on the same land. I am sure my owner will be happy to receive you. Have a cup of tea and a samosa.'

I looked at Roopa but she was not listening to our conversation.

She took a handful of soil from the little patch of garden in front of the hotel and said, 'This is my land. This is my soil. My ancestors made this their home. They were born and burnt here. The land, the trees, the air, the water everything was ours. We knew the customs, the culture and the food. One day, some person drew a line and created two nations. And suddenly we became foreigners in our own land. We had to leave and adopt some other place whose language, food and culture were alien to us. A single line made me a stranger to my own land. People who have been uprooted have a special pain which no one else can understand.'

I was quiet. I could only imagine her agony. I held her hand and suddenly realized that the bouquet of flowers I had meant to give to the owners of her old house was lying on the front seat of the car, withering slowly in the December sunshine.

One day, I had to take an auto to get to some place. These days in Bangalore, like other big cities, one is held completely at the mercy of the auto drivers. It is up to them, whether they want to take us or not. And even if we do get one, we have to keep all our fingers crossed till we reach our destination safely. It is rare to find a driver who does not drive his auto like a race car, or has a meter which gives the correct reading.

Anyway, that day I had asked various passing autos but none was ready to take me, so I was standing by the roadside. Suddenly a car stopped a little further ahead and someone rolled down one of the windows and waved at me. Looking carefully, I realized it was my friend Saroja. She was gesturing to me, indicating that I should get into the car. But I was hesitant. I said, 'I'm going towards the airport, it will be too far for you.'

But Saroja was firm, 'Please get in first. This is not a parking area. I too am going towards the airport to my hospital. It will not be out of my way.'

Saroja and I have been friends for a long time now, though our ways of looking at life are completely different. However, we have always maintained a transparency in our views, which has kept the friendship alive. It also helps that Saroja is an open-minded person, and does not hesitate to tell me her opinions. Sometimes we get into arguments, but talking frankly with one another helps to patch things up.

'What are you doing without a car? Why were you waiting for an auto?' Saroja was clearly astonished to see me near an auto stand.

'My drivers are on leave, and I don't like driving on Bangalore's roads these days, so I thought I'll take an auto.'

'You could have taken a taxi!'

'What is wrong in taking an auto? Many people in this city don't own a car.'

'But autos are dangerous.'

'For that matter travelling by road is far more dangerous than travelling by air.'

'That is true, though these days planes never stick to their schedules. I feel sick of travelling.'

'Then you are lucky you don't have to travel too often, given your work at the hospital.'

Saroja and her husband run a small hospital that has been quite successful. Both their sons are married. One stays abroad, while the younger one stays with them with his family. They have a big house, and Saroja is well settled with few worries. Or so I thought!

Without replying to me, Saroja stared outside, frowning.

'What is the matter? You seem unhappy,' I asked.

'To be honest, I am unhappy in the hospital and at home.'

'Why? Everything is so good for you.'

'That is what you think. But at home, my mother-in-law expects me to do everything. She forgets that I am also growing old. My daughter-in-law wants me to look after the grandchildren and manage the home, while she goes out to work. No one understands that as we grow older, we lose the patience to manage everything like we did in our younger days. I am caught between two generations.'

'Saroja, all of us go through this dilemma at this age. We are neither as old-fashioned as our parents, nor as progressive as our sons and daughters-in-law.'

'Besides that my relatives keep bothering me. They come to the hospital for treatment and don't pay us a paisa. I wouldn't have minded that so much but they never even have a word of thanks for us. They behave as if it is their right. If I complain about this to my husband he gets upset.'

'How is your practice?' I tried to change the topic.

'Don't ask me. There is so much competition in Bangalore. It is very difficult to have a private practice and even worse if one's children are not doctors. Often I think it would be better if we just sold the hospital and kept the money in the bank. Nowadays even the patients are so inquisitive. The other day one asked me a dozen questions while I was examining him. They think we can perform miracles with the latest medicines and surgery. If they don't respond to treatment they start complaining that we are exploiting them.'

Saroja was in full flow. 'How is Milind?' I interrupted.

Milind is her son who is a software engineer in the US.

'Oh, life there is not easy. There is so much of retrenchment. He is always under the threat of unemployment. His wife is also working. And there is no domestic help in the US you see, so the children go to a creche. They have not learnt a word of Kannada. I feel sad.'

It was taking us almost half an hour to travel a couple of kilometers, as there were traffic snarls all around. I was scared Saroja would start complaining about the road and the traffic situation as well, so I quickly asked, 'How is your friend Vani?'

'Don't ask me about her. Now that they are doing so well in life, she looks down upon me. How can I continue to be friends with her?'

'How is Vimla?'

Vani and Vimla were Saroja's friends for many years. But now she seemed to have developed problems with both.

'Oh I hardly meet Vimla. She always has either health or financial problems. Who has the time to listen to her complaints?'

Finally I asked the question that was on my mind after hearing her endless worries. 'Saroja, according to you, what is a happy life?'

Saroja looked at me and laughed, probably at my ignorance.

'A perfect life would be one without any worries. Daughters-in-law would be obedient and friendly and mothers-in-law without any expectations from us. Older people would not be demanding and friends would be understanding. Relatives would appreciate our work, and patients would realize that the doctor always tries his or her level best, but are not gods. Everybody would strive for a better life.'

By then we had reached Airport Road and it was time for me to get out of the car. But I wanted to say something to her before that.

'Saroja you are dreaming of utopia. Your dream is an impossible one. If we want to be happy we have to change our attitude and not the world's! The world is full of difficulties and unfulfilled desires just as the earth is full of dust and mud. If you want to keep your feet clean in this muddy world, there are only two solutions. Either cover the entire earth or wear a pair of sandals.'

Saroja interrupted, 'What a great thought. Who told you this?'

By that time I was out of the car and closing the door behind me. I told her, 'I was not fortunate enough to hear these lines from the guru himself as he was born 2,500 years before me. He was the Buddha.'

'When did you become a Buddhist?'

'Just now, in front of you.'

17

Sweet Hospitality

Some years ago, my friend Suman came from the US to stay with me for a month. She had been living abroad for nearly twenty-five years. All her relatives and friends are in Bangalore and Dharwad, and the purpose of her visit was to catch up with all her friends. She had grown-up children who were not interested in visiting India, but she had the freedom to spend as much time as she wanted in her country. She still felt strongly about having her roots in India, perhaps more so because she had been away for so long.

Suman is very conscious of her health, and is always trying to keep her weight under control since she has a history of blood sugar and hypertension in her family. When I went to the US, I stayed with her once and saw her way of living. She diets, exercises, walks and meditates. She spends perhaps up to four hours a day on her fitness regime. When we were in school together she was on the plumper side and used to love eating sweets. Now, she hardly touches them. Knowing her love for them, I can understand the great effort she must be making to abstain from them. Once I asked her how she managed to do it. She replied sadly, 'It is so difficult. But

I practice it. Sometimes I feel like having sweets, which is why we don't keep any in the house.'

When Suman was staying with me, I accompanied her on some of her visits to the houses of friends and relatives. In India, a guest is supposed to be treated like god. Traditionally, the best of everything is put aside for the guest. People will go out of their way to make the guest happy. I have noticed that this is more so in the small towns and villages.

Once, I went with Suman to our friend Jaya's house. Jaya was not keeping well, but had gone to great efforts to prepare many eatables for us. As soon as we arrived, she disappeared into the kitchen and reappeared after a while bearing two tall copper glasses and two plates of sweets. They were all traditional home-made sweets and I could see the copious quantities of ghee and sugar oozing out of them. Jaya was serving us with great warmth and it was getting awkward to say no. In such situations, it is expected that the guest should finish all that has been put on the plate. In fact, it can be perceived to be an insult if food is left uneaten by the guest.

Suman was of course quite upset to see all the sweets being served. She could not afford to abandon her diet. Though it may be easy to stay off the food one has not seen in years, as soon as one is face to face with it, the food becomes irresistible. Temptation and Jaya's coaxing got the better of her and Suman ended up eating all the sweets. By the time we finished those, Jaya arrived bearing a second round of sweets.

'You must drink this payasa,' she said, putting before

us bowls filled to the brim with creamy appali payasa. 'It took me most of the afternoon to prepare this and I made it just for you.'

This time Suman was stronger and refused strictly. Since I was not on a diet, I finished my bowl, enjoying it immensely. It was indeed very good. Jaya was quite upset that Suman had refused the payasa.

'Come on Suman, please have it. We are not as well off as you are now, but I prepared it with a lot of love. You will never get this in the US. Now that you are in India you must forget your diet. Get back to it when you return home.'

By now Suman was in tears. Seeing her state, I told Jaya, 'Don't insist so much. You have made everything with a lot of affection, but let her decide what she wants to eat.'

Jaya was unhappy that I had spoken for Suman. 'If I insist she will have it. This is supposed to be good for health. I knew your grandfather, Suman, and he used to love this payasa. He was a friend of my grandfather's and I remember him well. He was as thin as a stick, even though he used to eat everything, including sweets, and never dieted in his life.'

'That is true. But my grandfather lived in a village and used to work in the paddy fields. He used to walk ten miles a day. That would have burned up all the calories he ate. My grandmother used to walk to the well and fetch water even in her old age. Theirs was a different way of life, our pattern of living has changed completely. Please understand.'

Our visit to Jaya's house ended on a sad note. And as Suman went visiting from house to house, the same story was repeated. At the end of her stay, Suman showed me the reading on the weighing scale. She had put on five kgs. She left India full of worries about how it would affect her health, and not the happy memories she had expected to take back with her.

Her parting words got me thinking. She said, 'People do not understand that hospitality does not mean serving rich food and large helpings. In all the houses I visited, they were upset that I refused to eat so much. For them it was a courtesy, but for me it is like poison. When I went to Delhi, I attended a wedding where they had a separate section with sugar-less food. I thought that was so considerate of the hosts. Nowadays everyone is conscious of one's health and wants to eat healthy food. For me some kinds of food are silent killers and I have to avoid them. I wish my friends had understood this and not taken offence.'

I listened to Suman and felt sad. She was correct. Hospitality means making a person feel at home, allowing her to relax and sharing whatever we have without making anyone uncomfortable. But we seem to have forgotten that. For us hospitality means preparing masses of food and piling up the guest's plate with it. And if she refuses, we get annoyed and jump to conclusions.

As I waved goodbye to Suman, I could only wish that Indian hospitality did not remind her always of a plate of sweets!

18

FRIENDS FOREVER

Radha and Rohini were my students through their college days. They were inseparable friends and I learnt they had studied together since the first year of school. I have rarely seen two friends who were so close to each other. They took all their classes together, attended lab with each other and were horrified when I suggested they take different lab partners as I was in favour of my students changing their lab partners every semester so they could learn to work with different kinds of people.

Of the two Rohini was the quieter one. She was also very talented and could paint and embroider beautifully. In fact often she would stitch similar clothes for herself and Radha and people would think they were sisters. There was such perfect understanding between them that they never felt the need to make other friends. I would see them together and wonder what would happen to their friendship later in life and after they got married. As it turned out, Radha got married first, to Ramesh, a civil engineer, and moved to Delhi. Rohini married Suresh, a mechanical engineer and set up house in Bangalore itself. I would see her once in a while and ask her about Radha. Time passed and both had children.

Meanwhile, I got more involved in my work with the foundation. In the course of that, I was planning to build an orphanage in the outskirts of the city. My funds were limited, so I was looking for someone who would take on the task of building the place at cheaper rates and yet do good work. Cheap is not always the best, is what I found out soon enough.

One day, a man in his late thirties came to meet me. He gave me a wonderful quotation for the work. He had made out a detailed proposal and I was very impressed. So I asked him, 'How will you do all this at the rate you have specified? Won't you be incurring a loss?'

He smiled and replied, 'Madam, this is something I want to do. It is not a business proposition. I am not making any profit on this.'

I was pleased to hear his answer and said, 'It is always good to see young people getting involved in social projects. So are you a philanthropher too?'

Now he grinned widely and answered, 'Actually someone very close to me wanted me to take on this work. I don't know if you remember her but she talks about you very often. Her name is Radha and she is my wife.' Now it all became clear to me. It also explained the name of his construction firm, Radha Constructions.

'Of course I remember Radha. But I thought you were in Delhi? Have you moved here?'

'I left my job and started my own construction company in Delhi. It is doing very well and recently we moved here as I want to expand my work in Bangalore. Since Radha is from Bangalore, she too was keen to come back and stay here for a few years. Soon after we moved she read in the papers about your work and also about this orphanage that you plan to build. She immediately asked me to draft a proposal and meet you with it. You know, it is my belief that Radha has brought me a lot of good luck after our marriage. There was no way I could refuse her.'

I was delighted to hear his story, and especially that he attributed his success to my former student. 'Will you tell her to come and meet me?' I blessed her in my mind, for asking her husband to do this work for us at no profit.

Radha came to meet me the very next day. Of course she looked much older now. I was glad to see the happiness on her face. There is no greater joy for a teacher than to meet an old student who is doing well in life and is satisfied. Invariably, Rohini's name came up in our conversation. 'So do you now dress in similar saris? Are your children as close friends as you two were at their age?'

To my surprise, Radha remained quiet. Then she said, 'I don't know why but Rohini has changed a lot. You know I was so keen to come back to Bangalore because of her too. She was almost like a sister to me. And I know that was the way she felt about me as well. But somehow, things have changed. Our friendship is not the same any more.'

Astonished at her story, I asked Radha to explain further. She said, 'Rohini has changed a lot. Whenever I go to visit her she is very polite, but the warmth is missing. She talks to me like she would to a stranger, and not her oldest friend. I have been trying to work out the reason, but I am still at sea.'

After talking for a while longer, Radha went back home. I felt I should talk to Rohini. Having been their teacher I still thought of them as my students. Teachers tend to be under the illusion that their students will always listen to them! So, I sent word for Rohini. She came to meet me at my office. I was seeing her after many months and was shocked to see her state. There were worry lines on her face, and she looked tired.

I tried talking cheerfully to her, 'So Rohini what have you painted lately? Do you remember how you always used to pester me to give you a sari which you could embroider? Well, Radha gave me a plain sari yesterday. Will you make something on it?'

Quietly Rohini replied, 'No Madam. I have stopped doing all that.'

'What is the matter with you Rohini? You seem to be under a lot of stress. I came to know from Radha that you are no longer friendly with her? Did she do something to hurt you?'

'Not really. You see, now there is a lot of difference in Radha's and my economic situations. Her husband is doing well, whereas we are having a lot of financial problems. I don't think it is possible for people of unequal status to be friends. Now that Radha is rich she pities me.'

'Why do you say so? Did she say anything to you?'

'Whenever she comes she brings expensive toys for my daughter and presents me with silk saris at the least pretext. She knows I cannot reciprocate. Perhaps she looks down at me and I am not comfortable around her. So I have tried to keep a distance between us.'

Now I understood. And Radha was not even aware of all this! I explained quietly to Rohini, 'Come on. You must realize that in a true friendship the status does not matter. It is what you make of the situation. If Radha had given your daughter cheap toys you would have said she is doing so because you are poor. It is not what Radha does, but what your interpretation of it is. You must have read of the friendship between Krishna and Sudama. One was poor and the other a king, yet they kept their friendship alive. Radha gives you what she can afford and you too can try to give her something within your means. It need not be expensive. You are so talented. You can give her some paintings, or make a dress for her child. It is not the price but the thought behind a gift that matters. Don't spoil your friendship of so many years because of an inferiority complex. Give Radha a chance. Shall I tell you an interesting line that I read somewhere once?'

Rohini was sitting quietly listening to me and nodded her head.

'I was born with relatives, but at least I can choose my friends!'

We both burst out laughing. Rohini went home looking much happier and a few days later I received a beautiful sari with intricate thread work done all over it. The card read, 'From Radha and Rohini'.

Many years ago, I was heading a project in the company where I was working. My team consisted of mostly married women of similar age and background. We were given one big hall to sit in. I had a cabin with a glass partition, while the others sat outside. During lunch hours the women would sit outside and gossip. They were just loud enough for me to hear them from behind my partition and I would end up listening to the stories of their households.

Most of the women were quite talkative, except for one called Neeta. And while the rest used to usually complain about their husbands and in-laws, Neeta would be the only one who had anything positive to say about her family.

When Neela would grumble about her mother-in-law, Neeta would say, 'My mother-in-law is like my mother.' Then Kusuma would say, 'My sister-in-law is so jealous of me.' And Neeta could be heard saying, 'My sister-in-law is fantastic. We share everything like sisters.' Geeta's husband had a short temper and she would talk about how he got angry about the smallest issues. But Neeta would say she was more short-tempered than her husband, in fact he hardly ever lost his temper.

One day Neeta came to the office wearing a very pretty pink sari. Everyone commented what a lovely sari it was and I asked her, 'Where did you buy it from? Is it your birthday?' Neeta blushed and replied, 'Yes, madam, it is a birthday gift from my husband.'

And so we heard stories of her perfect family everyday. Whereas everyone had the standard complaints of all working women, on how they had to juggle their office work and responsibilities at home, where they got little support from their husbands or in-laws, Neeta would relate how her father-in-law helped out the kids with their homework, and how her husband helped her in the kitchen.

It was the common consensus that Neeta was a lucky person, perhaps even the eighth wonder of the world. Savitri, the poetess, said, 'Neeta's family is better even than the flawed moon—it does not have any defects!'

Those days of laughter and joking passed and slowly the group dissolved and each went their own way. Many years later, I got a call from Neeta. For some time I could not place her but then slowly her stories came back to me. She was Mrs Perfect! She spoke softly into the phone and I thought I heard a trace of anxiety in her voice. She wanted to come and meet me one day and I told her to do so.

The day she stepped into my office I was astonished to see her state. While her friends had progressed from youth to middle age, Neeta seemed to have jumped straight to old age. She was frail and her hair had greyed. We talked for a while about our old team members, but she had no

idea where they were now. So I told her. Neela, who used
to fight with her mother-in-law and had moved out of the
house with her husband, had finally gone back and looked
after the old lady in her illness. Kusuma had helped out
her 'jealous' sister-in-law when she was in trouble and
Geeta's husband had mellowed down with age and was
now a pleasant, jovial person to talk to.

Life had gone round like a wheel for most of these
people. They had taken on the challenges and
responsibilities that came with age and had faced them
with courage. Then I asked Neeta, 'So how are you now?
You never had the troubles that these people had.'

She looked even sadder at my words and there were
tears in her eyes. 'Madam you don't know the problems I
am facing.'

'You and problems, Neeta?'

'Yes Madam. I am suffering from depression. I have
to go to the psychiatrist.'

'There is nothing wrong with that Neeta. It is good
that you are taking a doctor's help to overcome your
condition. It is like going to a doctor for any other ailment,
there is nothing to worry about there.'

'Madam, I have been depressed for so long that the
psychiatrist says if I shared it with someone I know and
respect, it might help me. That is why I asked to meet
you.'

'I am glad you thought of me Neeta, but why are you
so depressed? You had such a wonderful family life.'

'I always had lots of problems. I just could never bring
myself to talk about them. My mother-in-law and sister-

in-law were worse than Neela's and Kusuma's. My husband always took their side in any argument. I was so miserable. When my friends would talk about their families I always wished I could share my story with them, but my mother had told me never to talk ill of my family in public. She said I should always restrain my emotions and whatever happens at home, should put up a happy face outside it. As a result I would pretend to be happy. For me being frank meant showing my weakness.'

I was stunned by her words. I had always thought being frank was a virtue. I was taught to look around me at all the misery that existed in the world and then compare others' problems with my own. I had counted my blessings when I felt sad and that had kept me going even in my darkest days.

Meanwhile Neeta was still pouring out her heart. 'Do you remember that pink sari I wore one day which everyone commented on and said was so pretty? Even you had asked me where I got it from. I lied that it was a birthday gift from my husband. He has never given me anything on my birthdays. Nobody helped me with my children's homework or in the kitchen. I would struggle all alone trying to do everything. My life was no different from my colleagues', but at least they gave themselves the freedom to talk about it and comment in public. I was too busy trying to show I had a perfect life.'

'Now that you have realized that did not work, forget the past and try to be happy.'

'Nothing comes free. I paid a heavy price trying to keep up the pretence of my life. I suffered from repeated bouts of depression. I tried talking about this with some people but they did not understand and I heard some make nasty comments about me. I hope you understand why I have come to you today and told you the truth.'

I took Neeta's hand in mine and said to her, 'Everyone has secrets. We all have faults that we try to hide. But the problem arises when we don't acknowledge those troubles and faults even to ourselves and pretend to be what we are not. A peacock looks beautiful when it dances but it cannot sing. A cuckoo is dark but has a golden voice. That is why a cuckoo should never dance and a peacock should not try to sing! We can live our lives in happiness only when we acknowledge our difficulties and failures and try to overcome them with our strength of character.'

20

HUNDRED PER CENT FREE

At the Infosys Foundation, we get hundreds of letters every day asking for monetary help for all kinds of purposes—for higher education, a wedding, medical help and so on. Usually we try to verify the genuineness of the claim and then we give sixty to eighty per cent of the total money required by the person. Once I got a letter from someone I had offered to pay a part of the money he required. He said, 'You are very hard-hearted. Why can't you give me the entire amount that I have asked for?' I do so because two incidents in my life taught me that sometimes it is better to let a person struggle. It provides an incentive to strive harder. Anything given away for free loses value and is not treated with the respect it deserves.

A few years back, when I looked out of my office window, I used to see a young boy of about fourteen selling dusters at the traffic light. He was thin as a stick and dressed in rags. I used to compare his state with the smartly-dressed children sitting in school buses, carrying their bags of books and would feel bad at the boy's deprivation. One day, I decided to do something about it and called him up to my office. He walked in looking scared and diffident. I offered him some coffee and biscuits to make him feel at ease. Initially he was feeling too awkward to eat. But slowly, he relaxed and after drinking the coffee answered my questions.

His name was Ravi and his father was a coolie and his mother a housemaid. He studied in a local school and in the morning hours he sold car dusters to earn some money for his education.

I asked, 'How much money do you make every month?'
He said, 'Between thirty to forty rupees a month'
'Can I see your progress card?'
The next day the boy came with his progress card. He was doing well in school and was obviously a bright child. So I said, 'Suppose I gave you fifty rupees a month, then you would not need to sell dusters in the morning. Instead you can use the time to do your homework or learn something else.' The boy was taken aback at the proposition and looked at me uncomprehendingly. So I said, 'Just suppose I am buying all your stock of cloth every month and also giving a few rupees extra. That would mean you are earning Rs 50. Use it to study further. But I will want to see your progress report every three months before giving you the money.' Now he understood and agreeing to my idea he left with great joy written on his face.

Thereafter he came to my office every three months and after showing his card he would leave with the money. His progress report showed he was doing well in school. One day, he asked to speak to me. I was happy to see a smart, confident young boy in front of me. He came straight to the point, 'Madam, now my stipend should be increased to Rs 100 per month.'

'Why do you say so?'

'Madam, two years back each duster was for Rs 2. Now it is Rs 4. So, you should pay me Rs 100 per month.'

I looked at him in surprise. Obviously he looked at the money he got from me each month as his due and did not feel the need to work himself to earn more.

Another incident soon after that convinced me to start my policy of extending only part of the help where money was concerned.

I am very fond of atlases. When I was growing up in a village, it was difficult to get hold of one. So when I started the foundation I decided to start distributing atlases free to school libraries. In them children could see the country and the world and learn the vastness of the planet they lived in. I thought it was the perfect way to open a child's eyes to the immense variety of life on earth. Later, teachers used to come to my office and collect them free for their schools.

Once I was spending some time in the rural parts of Karnataka on work. It was dusk and the cattle were coming back after their day's grazing. There was a pall of dust everywhere and I smelled the wonderful aroma of fresh groundnuts in the air. A man was sitting with a pile of freshly plucked groundnuts in front of the local school gate. It was quite irresistible and I went up to him and asked for a kilo. The man was a farmer selling his product directly to customers passing that way.

He weighed a kilo and gave it to me loose. 'Take this and put it in your bag,' he said. I was not carrying one, so I asked him to get one from somewhere. He thought for a minute then he turned to his assistant and said, 'Run into the school, the classrooms are still open. There will be a big red book there, with thick pages. Tear out one page and get it.' Before I could protest the boy had run into the school. Soon he came holding a colourful page and I was handed my kilo of groundnuts in it. I looked closely at the page and realized it was from one of the atlases I had given to the school some months back! I was shocked.

'Why did you tear the page from this book?' I asked. The man answered, 'Oh some lady gives these book free to the school. The paper is nice and thick, so we use it sometimes for wrapping things.'

Then seeing the shocked look on my face he said placatingly, 'We do it only when we need paper in a hurry, not otherwise.'

I looked down sadly at the pack of groundnuts in my hand. In that dim light, I was sure I could make out the seal of our foundation on it.

21

TWO FACES OF POVERTY

Leela has been working in my office for many years. She sweeps, dusts and mops. She does her work quietly and takes on any extra work without any complaints. Since she was always so quiet and I was usually very busy, I did not know much about her personal life, apart from the fact that her husband had deserted her and she was bringing up three daughters singlehandedly.

One day, she came in to clean my office and after doing her work, stood hesitantly in front of me. It was such an uncharacteristic thing for her to do, that I was surprised. Slowly, she brought out a soiled bundle and put it in front of me. Then she said in a low voice, 'Madam can you lend me twenty thousand rupees?' I was still puzzled and asked, 'What happened Leela? Why do you suddenly need so much money?' She replied, 'My youngest daughter wants to join college and I need the money for that.' While she was explaining I opened the cloth bundle. Inside, there was a pair of worn out gold bangles. 'Why are you giving this to me Leela?' I asked.

'These are the only assets I have. I will do anything to see my daughter studies further. She is very bright. She wants to become an engineer.'

I could make out the pride in her voice when she spoke of the girl. But when has a child not seemed the best and the brightest to her mother? So I told Leela, 'Take back these bangles. I am not a moneylender. I want to meet your daughter and talk to her myself. Ask her to come and meet me with her school marks cards.'

The next day a pretty girl in ordinary but clean clothes was waiting for me in the office. Her face was bright with intelligence and as soon as I entered she stood up politely.

'Madam I am Leelamma's daughter,' she introduced herself. 'My name is Girija. My mother said you wanted to talk to me.'

Then she placed her marks cards in front of me. I was taken aback to see the high marks she had scored consistently. She also had numerous extra-curricular activity certificates. No wonder Leela was so proud of her and wanted to pledge her bangles for her. I looked again at her closely. She was fair and her face was as clear as dew. That seemed strange, as Leela was short and dark. We talked for a few more minutes and I could make out Girija's fondness for her mother and sisters in her words. I sent her back and called Leela.

'Leela, I met your other two daughters when they came to the office some times, but I am very impressed after meeting Girija. There is something about her that sets her apart. You were right, she is very bright. I will help you out with the fees. If she performs well I will give her entire course fees. She has it in her to change her future, if she continues to work hard . . .' I was talking while clearing my desk and only after I had spoken for so long I realized that Leela was standing without saying a word. Finally she said, 'I need to tell you something before you proceed further with your help. Girija is not my child. I have adopted her.' I was amazed. 'When? Why?' I asked.

She sighed. 'It is a long story. Many years ago I was working for a young girl. She was staying by herself. Her parents were in the US and she was supposed to go to them after finishing her studies. I was a cook in the house. The girl was good looking and quite friendly. Often boys and girls would be at her house and there was a lot of fun, music, laughter and partying.

'One day I found the girl looking worried and sad. She would often talk to me so I asked her what the matter was. She confessed that she was pregnant. The boy who was responsible had gone abroad soon after hearing the news and she was left in the lurch. She did not dare tell her parents and it was too late for an abortion.

'What could I do after hearing such a story? I looked after her through her pregnancy, cooking the best foods. She gave birth to a baby girl in a nursing home here. All the while no one but me knew about the situation. Soon after the baby was born she told me to take it and put it in an orphanage. I tried, but holding the tiny baby in my arms I found myself unable to give her away and decided to bring her up. I already had two daughters and my husband had deserted me, but I knew I would always find enough to share with this new soul. That girl is Girija.'

I was dumbstruck by Leela's story and her courage

and generosity. The crushing poverty of her life had not diminished the humanity within her.

Yet not all children are fortunate enough to find a Leela to take care of them. There are others whose stories of cruelty and neglect can amaze even the most cynical of people. One such unfortunate child was Somnath.

Usually I try not to give money to individual parents. Instead, we give it to a hospital where they take care of the needy at nominal rates. Once I made an exception and have regretted it ever since. It started one day when Ramappa came to meet me. He was standing in the reception arguing with my secretary who did not want to let him in without an appointment. Since he was already there I saw no point in turning him away and asked him in. His son, he said, was suffering from cancer and needed urgent surgery. He was a clerk and could in no way afford the Rs 2 lakh needed. I looked at all the papers and medical certificates he had got with him. Then I told him to get some more papers—proof of hospitalization, pathological report, estimation of the operation, his id in the hospital, etc. I also wanted the doctor's name so I could talk to him.

Ramappa thought for a while, then said, 'All right I will bring the papers tomorrow.' But the next day, Ramappa turned up holding a child by the hand. The boy was obviously very sick and it made a pathetic sight. I was furious that he had dragged the child all the way to my office in this condition. 'Why did you get him?' I asked. 'I only wanted to see some papers.'

Ramappa was ready with his reply. 'It would take me

a few days to get all the papers you wanted, so I got the child as proof.'

I felt sorry for Somnath and wrote out a cheque for Rs 25,000. Ramappa said, 'Can you give me a letter that you have given me this money? I can show it to other donors. If they see your name they too will agree to help me.' I could see nothing wrong in writing such a letter and gave it to him. Ramappa thanked me wholeheartedly and went away promising to let me know how the operation went. But there was no news from him and a year passed. We too forgot about Ramappa till the auditors were doing their work and I realized that Ramappa had not called nor sent any other papers or receipts of the operation. I called up the hospital he had mentioned and wanted to know if they had operated on any child called Somnath that year. I was sad to hear that they hadn't. Perhaps Ramappa could not raise all the money, I thought and berated myself for not helping him more or following up on the case.

I decided to go and meet him. I still had the address he had given me. When I found the place, it was locked. It was a big, three-storeyed building in the latest style with plenty of tiles and granite. It was by far the grandest house in the locality. Having come so far I did not want to go without finding out more about Somnath, so I knocked on the next door. An old lady came out and was least taken aback to find a stranger at her door asking questions. She talked freely to me.

'Where are Ramappa and Somnath?' I asked her.

'Somnath died six months ago.'

I was saddened, but not surprised.

The old woman was meanwhile chatting away. 'Somnath's disease came as a boon for Ramappa. He got a letter from some famous lady who gave him 25,000 rupees for the operation. With that he went around to other donors and managed to raise Rs 8 lakh. He used the money to build this new house and also started an auto business. Now he is doing very well in life.'

'But didn't he get Somnath's operation done?'

'Ramappa was no fool to get him operated. He was least bothered about it. In the end, he used to carry him around when he went to collect the money. Poor Somnath suffered a lot and died at home.'

I was dumbstruck. By then a man appeared from inside and told the old woman not to talk. But she replied fiercely, 'Why should I not talk? I saw Somnath from the day he was born. I saw him suffer. God will certainly not forgive Ramappa for what he did to his own son.'

I had got to know enough by then and took my leave. I found myself in tears as I walked to the car. All I could do was thank god there are still people like Leela in this world. They lessen the pain and suffering inflicted by people like Ramappa, of whom unfortunately there are plenty.

22

INDIA, THE HOLY LAND

Maya was a simple young lady who lived in the Tibetan settlement in the outskirts of Mundugod, near Hubli in north Karnataka. She used to teach the Tibetan language to the children in the camp, so they would not forget their roots. She was smart and hard working.

My father was a doctor working in Hubli and he occasionally visited that settlement. If any of the Tibetans wanted further treatment, they would visit my father at the Government Hospital in Hubli. Maya too started visiting my father when she was expecting her first child.

Over the months she became quite friendly with all of us. Whenever she came to the hospital she would pay us a visit too. My mother would invite her for a meal and we would spend some time chatting.

In the beginning, we would be in awe of her and stare at her almost-white skin, dove eyes, the little flat nose and her two long, thin plaits. Slowly we accepted her as a friend and she graduated to become my knitting teacher. Her visits were sessions of knitting, chatting and talking about her life in the camp and back in her country for which she still yearned. Maya would describe her homeland to us with great affection, nostalgia and at times, with tears in her eyes.

'Tibetans are simple people. We are all Buddhists but our Buddhism is of a different kind. It is called Vajrayana. There's been a lot of influence from India, particularly Bengal, in our country and religious practices. Even our script resembles Bengali.'

Her words filled me with a sense of wonder about this exotic land called Tibet and I would pester her to tell me more about that country. One day we started talking about the Dalai Lama.

'What is the meaning of Dalai Lama?' I asked.

'It means "ocean of knowledge". Ours is a unique country where religious heads have ruled for 500 years. We believe in rebirth and that each Dalai Lama is an incarnation of the previous one. The present Dalai Lama is the fourteenth . . . You know, India is the holy land of Buddha. Historically, we have always respected India. There is a nice story about how Buddhism came to Tibet through India . . .'

I could not wait to hear about this!

'Long ago there was a king in Tibet who was kidnapped by his enemies. They demanded a ransom of gold, equal to the weight of the king. When the imprisoned king heard this, he somehow sent word to his son, "Don't waste any gold to get me back. Instead, spend that money to bring good learned Buddhist monks from India. With their help, open many schools and monasteries so that our people can live in peace and gain knowledge".'

Months passed and Maya delivered a baby. After that

our meetings became less frequent. But she succeeded in awakening within me a curiosity about Tibet and a great respect for Buddhism

Recently I got a chance to visit Tibet and memories of Maya filled my mind. I knew I would be seeing a Tibet filled with Chinese but nevertheless I was keen to go. Among the places I wanted to see was a Buddha temple at Yerlong valley which she had described to me.

When I finally reached the valley, it was past midday. There was a cold wind blowing though the sun was shining brightly. The Brahmaputra was flowing like a stream here, nothing like the raging torrent in Assam. Snow-capped mountains circled the valley and there was absolute silence all around.

The monastery at Yerlong is supposed to be a famous pilgrimage spot, but I could see only a handful of people in the entire place. After seeing everything inside I sat down on the steps and observed the serene beauty of the place.

I noticed an old woman accompanied by a young man walking into the monastery. The woman was very old, her face was wrinkled and she walked slowly and weakly. She was wearing the traditional Tibetan dress and her hair was plaited. The young man on the other hand was dressed in the usual modern manner, in tight jeans and a body-hugging t-shirt. The woman started circumambulating the monastery using her stick for support while the man sat down on the steps like me.

When she finished, I realized the old lady was staring at me. Then she said something to the young man in

Tibetan. She looked tired by the end of her ritual and sat down on the steps. She said something to her companion again but he took little notice of her. So she slowly picked up her stick and came towards me. She sat down near me, took my hands and saying something, she gently raised my hands to her eyes and then kissed them. Before I could say anything, she got up and started to walk away. But I noticed she was smiling, as if she had achieved a long-held desire. I realized there was a wetness where her eyes had touched my hand.

Now the young boy reluctantly came up to me and apologised. 'Please forgive my grandmother,' he said. 'She is from a village in the interior part of Tibet. She has never ventured out of her village. This is the first time she has come to Yerlong. I beg your pardon for her behaviour.'

He was talking to me in English with an Indian accent.

'How come you speak English like us?' I asked in surprise.

'My name is KeTsang. I was in India for five years. I studied at Loyola College in Chennai. Now I run a restaurant in Lhasa. People here like Indian food and movies. I accompanied my grandmother for her pilgrimage. She was thanking you.'

'But for what? I have not done anything for her!'

'That is true, but your country has. It has sheltered our Dalai Lama for so many years. He is a living God to us, particularly to the older generation. We all respect the Dalai Lama, but due to political reasons, we cannot express it in public. You might have seen that there isn't a single photo of his in any public place in the whole of

Lhasa. He is the fourteenth, but we have paintings, statues and pictures only up to the thirteenth.'

I still did not understand the old lady's gesture. The grandson explained, 'She said, "I am an old lady and don't know how long I will live. If I don't thank you before I die, I will never attain peace. Let anyone punish me for this, it does not matter. It is a gift that I met an Indian today and was able to thank you for sheltering our Dalai Lama. Yours is truly a compassionate land."'

Her words eerily echoed Maya's from many years back. I could only look down at the wet spot on my hand and smile.

23

MOTHER'S LOVE

I was once invited to speak on motherhood at a seminar. It was a well-attended seminar and people from different walks of life had gathered. Some were medical practitioners, others were from orphanages, adoption agencies, and NGOs. Religious heads, successful mothers (the definition of which, according to the organizers, were those whose children had done well in life and earned lots of money), young mothers, all were there.

There were numerous stalls selling baby products, books on motherhood, on how to handle adolescents etc. The speakers were good and most of the time they spoke from the heart about their experiences. The media was present in full force, clicking away photos of celebrities. Since this had been organized by the social welfare department, there were many government officials and a big gathering of students too.

When my turn came, I started narrating an incident that I had been witness to many years ago.

Manjula was a cook in a friend, Dr Arati's house. Manjula's husband was a good-for-nothing. She had five children and when she became pregnant for the sixth time, she decided to get it aborted. She also decided to get a tubectomy done.

Dr Arati, however, came up with a different idea. Her sister was rich but childless and wanted to adopt a newborn baby. She was desparately searching for one, so Arati gave a suggestion.

'Manjula, instead of aborting the baby, why don't you deliver it, and irrespective of the gender, my sister will adopt it. She does not even stay in this city so you won't need to see the baby's face ever. She will adopt it legally and help you with the education of your remaining children too. This child, which is now unwanted, will be brought up well with lots of love. Think it over, the decision is yours and I will not insist.'

Manjula thought for a couple of days and finally agreed to the proposal. In a few months she delivered a baby girl. Dr Arati's sister also arrived that day after completing all the formalities. It had been decided that she would take the baby a day after it was born. But when the time came to hand over the child, Manjula refused to give her away. Her breasts were now full of milk and the baby had started feeding. She pressed the baby against her weak body and started crying, 'I agree that I am very poor. Even if I get a handful of rice, I will share that with this baby. But I cannot part with her. She is so tiny and so completely dependent on me. I am breaking my promise but I cannot live without my child. Please pardon me.'

Arati and her sister were naturally upset. They had prepared themselves to welcome this baby to their family. But seeing Manjula weep, they realized that motherhood may not always answer to the logic of agreements.

I concluded my speech saying that many times I have

seen a mother is ready to sacrifice anything for her children. Motherhood is a natural instinct. Our culture glorifies it and a mother is held in great respect, over anybody else. I was rewarded with great applause. I too was satisfied with my speech.

I stepped down from the podium, and saw Meera standing near by. She was blind and taught orphans in a blind school. She was representing her school at the seminar. I knew her fairly well because I visited her school often. I went up to her and said, 'Meera how are you?' She was quiet for a minute. 'I am fine, Madam. Can you do me a favour?'

'Tell me what is it?'

'Ahmed Ismail was supposed to pick me up and drop me to my school. But just now he called up on my cellphone and said that he is stuck in a traffic jam and will take more time. Can you drop me to my school?' Ahmed Ismail was a trustee of the blind school.

Meera's school was on my way to the office and so I agreed immediately. In the car, I noticed she was very quiet and so started the conversation.

'Meera, how was the seminar today? Did you like my lecture?'

I was expecting the usual polite answer, saying it was very good.

But Meera answered, 'I didn't like your lecture. Sorry for being so blunt, but life is not always like that.'

I was taken aback. I wanted to know the reason behind it and asked her, 'Tell me Meera. Why did you say that? What I narrated was a true incident and not a story.

Sometimes truth is stranger than fiction.'

Meera sighed, 'Yes, sometimes truth is stranger than fiction. That is really what I wanted to tell you. Let me tell you another story. There was once a five-year-old girl who was half-blind. Both her parents were labourers. The girl would complain often that she could not see clearly, but they would say that was because she wasn't eating properly and they would take her to the doctor when they managed to collect some money. One day, they finally took her to the doctor. He told them the girl needed an operation which cost a lot of money, else she would go blind slowly. The parents discussed something between themselves and took her to a bus-stand. They gave her a packet of biscuits and told her, "Child, eat the biscuits and we will be back in five minutes."

'For the first time in her life the child had got an entire packet of biscuits for herself. She was overjoyed and sat down to enjoy them. With her half blind eyes she could just make out her mother's torn red sari pallu disappear in the crowd. The day wore on, it started getting colder and she realized that it was getting dark. The packet of biscuits was over long back. She was alone, helpless and scared. She started calling for her parents and searched in vain for them, trying to spot the torn red pallu.'

'What happened after that?'

'The child continued to search for her parents, sleeping wherever she got a place. One day, a kind-hearted man saw her pitiable condition and took her to the blind school. The child could not give any address or name by which they could trace the parents. He requested the matron that in case any parent came forward to claim the child, they could hand her over after examining them. But nobody came looking for her. The child waited for her mother for several years, till one day she gave up all hope.'

I turned to Meera to see she was crying and I realized so was I. Even though I knew the answer in my heart, I asked her, 'Meera, how did you know all these details about that child?'

Through her tears, she replied, 'Because I was that half-blind child. Now, tell me, how could my mother leave me like that? She deceived me with a pack of biscuits. What happened to the motherhood that you spoke so strongly about? Is poverty more powerful than motherhood?'

I did not have any answer for her, but could only hold her hand in my own. I realized that there were as many kinds of mothers as there are people on this earth, and poverty can lead to acts of great desperation.

Even today, if I happen to see a woman on the road wearing a red sari, I think of Meera and her experience of motherhood.

One of my aims, when starting the Infosys Foundation, was to inculcate and spread the joy of reading among as many students and young children in the rural areas as possible. From my own experience of having grown up in a small town, I knew the best way to do this was to help schools and local libraries stock up on good books for children. It was in the course of identifying good government schools and youth clubs in the rural areas of Karnataka, that I happened to meet many young people from the small villages and towns of this state.

Krishna Murthy was a young man of about twenty who I met during my travels. He had recently graduated from a college in Bangalore. His father owned large properties and agricultural lands in the village and was therefore very well off. Krishna Murthy on the other hand, was taken in completely by the charms of city life and was intent on staying on in Bangalore rather than returning to his village as his father wanted. No amount of explaining could budge him. On the request of his father, I told him that life in a big city like Bangalore can be stressful, what with the rising costs of living, the high pollution levels, impossible traffic situation and water and electricity shortages. But young Krishna Murthy was adamant. Finally I told him about Guruprasad.

I met Guruprasad in my Bangalore office.

I had been very busy with my travels and been able to meet him only two months after he first said he wanted to talk to me about our library project. He had been very keen to meet only me. He was about twenty-three or twenty-four years of age and looked like any other young person these days, smartly dressed and equipped with the latest gadgets like cellphone, organizer etc. He was from a village called Kandale in Shimoga district. He had a jolly face and showed a great deal of spirit and enthusiasm. As we talked, I learnt that he had graduated with honours in English from a reputed college in Bangalore. A national level chess player, he was the eldest of two sons. His father was an agriculturist. After discussing his ideas for our library project, our conversation turned to Indian villages and life there.

'How do you spend your time in the village?' I asked him.

'Oh! There are numerous activities to keep me busy. I have a very lucrative mushroom business and everyday I have to work four to five hours on that. We have a big ancestral house. I live there with my parents and other relatives. In my village there is no pollution, though with better connectivity, we get almost all provisions usually available in cities close by. When I am not working at my business or looking after the house, I coach children in chess. We have also formed a youth club where along with my friends, I have started a library. The library has become a meeting point for many young people like me. We exchange ideas there and talk about which new books we should try to procure. I heard about your foundation's work there and came to meet you so we can take some books for our collection. I have been trying to start similar clubs and libraries in the neighbouring villages with the help of like-minded boys and girls.

'Life in our village is clean, healthy and I am happy being there as I am living the life I always wanted to.'

I was curious to know how much he was earning by his mushroom business.

'It depends upon how much you invest. If you invest ten rupees you can easily make forty rupees. It is better than any fluctuating share market. I earn much more than I would in Bangalore. I also don't need to spend enormous amounts of money commuting and paying exorbitant rents. I have a car which helps me a lot in my work. I don't feel inferior when talking to any city person. Nobody ever forced me to stay on in the village. It was my own decision and I am happy I took it.'

Guruprasad's words reminded me of one of Kuvempu's poems

Vasantha vanadali kooguva kogile
Raajana padaviya bayasuvudilla
Hoovina maradali jeenu hulugalu
Morevudu raajana bhayadindalla'
It is not in anticipation of the king's throne,
That in the springs, the cuckoo sings so beautifully
Nor is it out of fear of the king's anger
That the bees hum in the flower gardens

Guruprasad had decided on the course of his life by staying in his village and was happy there. He was doing what he enjoyed without giving in to any pressures but by using his own intelligence.

After hearing the story Krishna Murthy promised to think about staying on in his village. I don't know what he decided eventually and how happy he was with his decision. But till today I am convinced that it is young people like Guruprasad who can bring about change and a breath of fresh air to their villages. The future lies with him and many others like him.

May You Be the Mother of a Hundred Children

I was on my way to the railway station. I had the nine o'clock Bangalore-Hubli Kittur Express to catch. Halfway to the station our car stopped. There was a huge traffic jam. There was no way we could move either forward or reverse the car. I sat and watched helplessly as a few two-wheelers scraped past the car through a narrow gap. Finally I asked my driver what the matter was. Traffic jams are not uncommon but this was something unusual. He got out of the car and said the road ahead was blocked by some people holding a communal harmony meet. I now realized it was perhaps impossible to get to the station. The papers had reported about the meeting and had warned that the roads would be blocked for some time. The car was moved into a bylane and seeing there was no way I could try and make my way back home, I decided to join the crowd and listen to the speeches.

From a distance, I could see the dais. There were various religious heads sitting on a row of chairs on the stage. An elderly gentleman stood next to me and commented loudly, 'All this is just a drama. In India, everything is decided on the basis of caste and community. Even our elections are dictated by them. Whoever comes to power thinks only of the betterment of his community. It is easy to give speeches but in practical life they forget everything.'

Just then a middle-aged lady started speaking into the mike. From the way she was speaking, so confidently, it was apparent that she was used to giving speeches and had the gift of the gab. Her analogies were quite convincing. 'When you eat a meal, do you eat only chapattis or rice? No, you also need a vegetable, a dal and some curd. The tastes of the dishes vary, but only when they are put together do you get a wholesome meal. Similarly different communities need to live together in harmony and build a strong country . . .' etc. 'It is a nice speech but who follows all this in real life?' the gentleman next to me commented.

'Why do you say that?' I had to ask finally. He looked at me, surprised at my unexpected question, then answered, 'Because my family has suffered a lot. My son did not get a job as he was not from the right community, my daughter was transferred as her boss wanted to replace her with someone from his own community. It is everywhere. Wherever you go, the first thing people want to know is which caste or religion you belong to.'

The woman was still talking on the podium. 'What is her name?' I asked.

'She is Ambabhavani, a gifted speaker from Tamil Nadu.'

Her name rang a bell somewhere in my mind and

suddenly I was transported away from the jostling crowds and the loud speeches. I was in a time long past with my paternal grandmother, Amba Bai.

Amba Bai was affectionately called Ambakka or Ambakka Aai by everyone in the village. She spent her whole life in one little village, Savalagi, near Bijapur in north Karnataka. Like most other women of her generation she had never stepped into a school. She was married early and spent her life fulfilling the responsibilities of looking after a large family. She was widowed early and I always remember seeing her with a shaven head, wearing a red sari, the pallu covering her head always, as was the tradition in the then orthodox Brahmin society. She lived till she was eighty-nine and in her whole life she knew only the worlds of her ten children, forty grandchildren, her village and the fields.

Since we were farmers she owned large mudhouses with cows, horses and buffaloes. There was a large granary and big trees that cooled the house during the hot summers. There were rows of cacti planted just outside the house. They kept out the mosquitoes, we were told. Ajji (that's what we called Amba Bai) looked after the fields and the farmers with a passion. In fact, I don't recall her ever spending too much time in the kitchen making pickles or swects like other grandmothers. She would be up early and after her bath spend some time doing her daily puja. She would make some jowar rotis and a vegetable, and then head out to the fields. She would spend time there talking to the farmers about the seeds they had got, the state of the well or the health of their cattle. Her other passion in life was to help the women of the village deliver their babies.

Though I did not realize this till I was a teenager, Ajji was most unlike an orthodox Brahmin widow. She was very much for women's education, family planning and had much to say about the way society treated widows.

Those days there were few facilities available to the villages. There were a handful of medical colleges and not every taluk had a government hospital. In this scenario women who had borne children were the only help to others during childbirth. My grandmother was one of them. She was very proud of the fact that she had delivered ten perfectly healthy children, all of whom survived. And in turn, she would help others during their delivery irrespective of caste or community. She always had a word of advice or a handy tip for the various pregnant women of the village.

I would often hear various such nuggets from her. 'Savitri, be careful. Don't lift heavy articles. Eat well and drink more milk.'

'Peerambi, you have had two miscarriages. Be careful this time. Eat lots of vegetables and fruits. You should be careful but don't sit idle. Pregnancy is not a disease. You should be active. Do some light work. Send your husband Hussain Saab to my house. I will give some sambar powder. My daughter-in-law prepares it very well.'

Of course not everyone appreciated her advising them. One such person was Shakuntala Desai, who had stayed in the city for some time and had gone to school. 'What does Ambakka know about these things?' she would comment loudly, 'Has she ever gone to school or read a medical book? She is not a doctor.'

But Ajji would be least bothered by these comments. She would only laugh and say, 'Let that Shakuntala get pregnant. I will deliver the baby. My four decades of experience is better than any book!'

My father's job took us to various towns to live in, but we always came to Ajji's village during the holidays. They were joyous days and we would enjoy ourselves thoroughly.

Once, when we were at the village, there was a wedding in the neighbouring village. Ajji always refused to attend these social gatherings. That time, I too decided to stay back with her and one night there was only Ajji, me and our helper Dyamappa in that large house.

It was an unusually cold, moonless winter night in December. It was pitch dark outside. Ajji and I were sleeping together. Dyamappa had spread his bed on the front veranda and was fast asleep. For the first time that night, I saw Ajji remove her pallu from her head and the wisps of grey hair on her head. She touched them and said, 'Society has some such cruel customs. Would you believe that I once had thick long plaits hanging down my back? How I loved my hair and what a source of envy it was for the other girls! But the day your grandfather died, no one even asked my permission before chopping off that beautiful hair. I cried as much for my hair as for my husband. No one understood my grief. Tell me, if a wife dies, does the widower keep his head shaved for the rest of his life? No, within no time he is ready to be a groom again and bring home another bride!'

At that age, I could not understand her pain, but now, when I recall her words, I realize how helpless she must have felt.

After sometime she changed her topic. 'Our Peerambi is due anytime. I think it will be tonight. It is a moonless night after all. Peerambi is good and pious, but she is so shy, I am sure she will not say anything to anyone till the pain becomes unbearable. I have been praying for her safe delivery to our family deity Kallolli Venkatesha and also at the Peer Saab Darga in Bijapur. Everyone wants sons, but I do hope there is a girl this time. Daughters care for parents wherever they are. Any woman can do a man's job but a man cannot do a woman's job. After your Ajja's death, am I not looking after the entire farming? Akkavva, always remember women have more patience and common sense. If only men realized that . . .'

Ajji had so many grandchildren she found it hard to remember all their names. So she would call all her granddaughters Akkavva and grandsons Bala.

As Ajji rambled on into the night, there was a knock on the door. Instinctively Ajji said, 'That must be Hussain.' And indeed it was. Ajji covered her head again and forgetting her griefs about widowhood, she asked quickly, 'Is Peerambi in labour?'

'Yes, she has had the pains since this evening.'

'And you are telling me now? You don't understand how precious time is when a woman is in labour. Let us go now. Don't waste any more time.'

She started giving instructions to Hussain and Dyamappa simultaneously.

'Hussain, cut the cactus, take a few sprigs of neem. Dyamappa, you light two big lanterns . . .

'Akkavva, you stay at home. Dyamappa will be with you. I have to hurry now.'

She was gathering some things from her room and putting them into her wooden carry-box. By that time, the huge Dyamappa, with his large white turban on his head and massive moustaches appeared at the door bearing two lanterns. In the pitch darkness he made a terrifying picture and immediately brought to my mind the Ravana in the Ramayana play I had seen recently. There was no way I was going to stay alone in the house with him! I insisted I wanted to go with Ajji.

Ajji was impatient. 'Akkavva, don't be adamant. After all, you are a teenage girl now. You should not see these things. I will leave you at your friend Girija's house.' But like any other teenager, I was adamant and would not budge from my decision.

Finally Ajji gave up. She went to the puja room, said a quick prayer and locked the house behind her. Four of us set off in pitch darkness to Hussain saab's house. Hussain lead first with a lantern, Ajji, with me clutching on to her hand, followed and Dyamappa brought up the rear, carrying the other lantern.

We made our way across the village. Ajji walked with ease while I stumbled beside her. It was cold and I did not know the way. All the time Ajji kept up a constant stream of instructions for Hussain and Dyamappa.

'Hussain, when we reach, fill the large drums with water. Dyamappa will help you. Boil some water. Burn some coal. Put all the chickens and lambs in the shed. See that they don't come wandering around . . .'

Finally we reached Hussain's house. Peerambi's cries of pain could be heard coming from inside.

Hussain and Peerambi lived alone. They were poor farm labourers who worked on daily wages. Their neighbour Mehboob Bi was there, attending to Peerambi. Seeing Ajji she looked relieved. 'Now there is nothing to worry. Ambakka aai has come.'

Ajji washed her feet and hands and went inside the room with her paraphernalia, slamming the doors and windows shut behind her. Outside on the wooden bench, Hussain and Dyamappa sat awaiting further instructions from Ajji. I was curious to find out what would happen next.

Inside, I could hear Ajji speaking affectionately to Peerambi. 'Don't worry. Delivery is not an impossible thing. I have given birth to ten children. Just cooperate and I will help you. Pray to God to give you strength. Don't lose courage . . .' In between, she opened the window partly and told Hussain, 'I want some turmeric powder. I can't search in your house. Get it from Mehboob Bi's house. Dyamappa, give me one more big bowl of boiling water. Hussain, take a new cane tray, clean it with turmeric water and pass it inside. Dyamappa, I want some more burning coal . . .'

The pious gentle Ajji was a dictator now!

The next few hours were punctuated by Peerambi's anguished cries and Ajji's patient, consoling words, while Hussain sat outside tense and Dyamappa nonchalantly smoked a bidi. The night got dark and then it started getting lighter and lighter. The cock, locked in its coop, crowed and with the rising sun we heard the sounds of a baby's crying.

Ajji opened one window pane and announced, 'Hussain, you are blessed with a son. He looks just like your father Mohammed Saab. Peerambi had a tough time but God is kind. Mother and child are both safe and healthy.'

S-l-a-a-m . . . the door shut again. But this time outside we grinned at each other in joy. Hussain knelt down and said a prayer of thanks. Then he jumped up and knocked on the door, wanting to see the baby. It remained shut. Ajji was not entertaining any visitors till she was done.

'Your clothes are dirty,' she shouted from inside. 'First have a bath, wear clean clothes and then come in, otherwise you will infect the baby and mother.'

Hussain rushed to the bathroom, which was just a thatched partition and poured buckets of clean water from the well on himself.

Even after he rushed in, I could hear only Ajji's voice. 'Peerambi, my work is over. I have to rush home. Today is my husband's death ceremony. There are many rituals to be completed. The priests will arrive any time and I have to help them. I will leave now and if you want anything, send word through Hussain.

'Peerambi, to a woman, delivering a baby is like going to the deathbed and waking up again. Be careful. Mehboob Bi, please keep Peerambi's room clean. Don't put any new clothes on the baby. They will hurt him.

Wrap him in an old clean dhoti. Don't kiss the baby on his lips. Don't show the baby to everybody. Don't keep touching him. Boil the drinking water and immerse an iron ladle in that. Peerambi should drink only that water. I will send a pot of home made ghee and soft rice and rasam for Peerambi to eat . . . Now I have to go. Bheemappa is supposed to come and clean the garden today. If I am late, he will run away . . .'

By now she had allowed the window to be opened. I peeped in and saw the tired but joyous face of Peerambi and a tiny, chubby version of Mohammed Saab, Hussain's father, asleep on the cane tray. The neem leaves were hanging, the cactus was kept in a corner and the fragrance of the *lobana* had filled the entire room. Ajji also looked tired and there was sweat on her forehead. But she was cleaning her accessories vigorously in the hot water and wiping them before placing them carefully back in her wooden box.

Just as we were about to leave, Hussain bent down and touched Ajji's feet. In a choked voice he said, 'Ambakka aai, I do not know how to thank you. We are poor and cannot give you anything. But I can thank you sincerely from the bottom of my heart. You are a mother of a hundred children. You have blessed my son by bringing him into this world. He will never stray from the correct path.'

Ajji touched him on his shoulder and raised him. There were tears in her eyes too. She wiped them and said, 'Hussain, God only wants us to help each other in difficult times. Peerambi is after all like another Akkavva to me.'

By now the sun was up and I followed Ajji back home without stumbling. Dyamappa was strolling lazily far behind us. One doubt was worrying me and I had to clear it. 'Ajji, you have given birth only to ten children. Why did Hussain say you are a mother of hundred?'

Ajji smiled and adjusting the pallu that was slipping off her head because of her brisk walk, she said, 'Yes. I have given birth only to ten children but these hands have brought out a hundred children in our village. Akkavva, I will pray that you become the mother of a hundred children, irrespective of the number you yourself give birth to.'